W9-COX-407

A Journey with God in Time

A Journey with God

JOHN S. DUNNE

in Time

A SPIRITUAL QUEST

UNIVERSITY OF NOTRE DAME PRESS   •   NOTRE DAME, INDIANA

University of Notre Dame Press

Copyright © 2003 by University of Notre Dame
Notre Dame, Indiana 46556
www.undpress.nd.edu
All Rights Reserved

Published in the United States of America

The author and publisher wish to thank Rev. Timothy Scully, C.S.C.,
for his generous aid, which made possible the color pictures.

Library of Congress Cataloging-in-Publication Data
Dunne, John S., 1929–
A journey with God in time : a spiritual quest / John S. Dunne.
p.   cm.
Includes bibliographical references and index.
ISBN 0-268-02562-2 (cloth : alk. paper)
ISBN 0-268-02563-0 (pbk. : alk. paper)
1. Dunne, John S., 1929–.   2. Catholics—United States—Biography.
I. Title.
BX4705.D8792 A3 2003
282'.092—dc22

2003017884

∞ *This book is printed on acid-free paper.*

O Lord, go with me
and be my guide,
in my most need
be by my side:
if you are guiding me
I shall not want,
if you are guarding me
I shall not fear,
though I am walking
in the valley of the shadow
of my dying,
you are walking with me,
and when I am not
you will have taken me.

Contents

A Journey with God in Time

A Storyboat

"I wonder what sort of a tale we've fallen into."
—J. R. R. Tolkien

"Story is our only boat for sailing on the river of time," Ursula LeGuin writes in a story, "but in the great rapids and the winding shallows, no boat is safe."[1] I encountered the great rapids and the winding shallows recently when I had heart surgery. What did I learn from this? I ask myself. "I only know now how real these things are,"[2] Jung said of the great symbols after his own hospital experience. My life is a journey in time, I have long thought, and God is my companion on the way. But now I know how real these things can be, how real the journey can be, how real God's companionship can be.

"We can know more than we can tell,"[3] Michael Polanyi says, and so we can know more than we can tell in a story. We cannot tell all we know, dwelling on the particulars of our life. We can tell of our voyages and travels on the river of time, but we can know of the eternal in us. It is particularly when we encounter the great rapids and the winding shallows that we come to know the eternal. I see this pattern in the stages on my own life's way. Each time there is a storyboat for sailing on the river of time, and each time there is an encounter with the great rapids and the winding shallows in which I come to know the eternal, to know the God who is my companion on the way.

My first storyboat was from my grandfather's stories when I was a child of about five years. He used to tell stories on our front porch on summer evenings and children from all over the neighborhood used to gather there to sit at his feet and listen. I don't remember the stories, though I remember those first five years of my life while he was alive were happy years. The next ten years, after he died, were not so happy, and I found myself looking at people's faces, studying them, to see if they were happy and to learn from them the secret. I can only guess my grandfather's stories had happy endings, something that is of the essence of stories according to Tolkien. They were happy endings, I guess, and from our reaction of surprise and delight as children, I guess they were often surprise endings as in the stories of O. Henry.

My first encounter with the great rapids and the winding shallows on the river of time, therefore, was an encounter with unhappiness. It did not occur until after that first golden age when my grandfather, my mother's father, was alive. He was my first companion on the way and used to take me on walks and tell me the names of things,

> My grandfather
> would take me on a way
> that later I would walk alone,
> remembering a last
> time I had passed a loved
> red cedar and a mossyback along

the river running
—I would stop and point
to see what he would call them,
and whatever he called anything,
that was its name.[4]

God has become my companion on the way, I realize now, replacing my grandfather, but I already had a notion of God, I remember, while my grandfather was still alive. I associated God with sparrows, not that I believed God was a sparrow, but whenever I saw a sparrow I thought of God. And I saw them often, as sparrows are the most common of birds. Perhaps I had heard the Gospel verse, "Are not two sparrows sold for a farthing? and not one of them shall fall on the ground without your Father," or in Luke, "and not one of them is forgotten before God."[5] My concept of God was of Someone as harmless as a sparrow and yet existing everywhere, like sparrows, and caring about everyone and everything.

My first spoken sentence, my mother carefully recorded in my baby book, was "Pire bi," which she said meant "Fire bites." I didn't play with fire, but I used to play as a child at seeing and saying and doing what God is doing in the opening scene of the Bible, "Let there be light."[6] I had not yet come upon this idea in the Gospel of John, but was trying to reenact in play the story of creation in Genesis. I was like the boy Ray Bradbury describes in the opening scene of *Dandelion Wine*, evoking the sunrise. God creates by letting be, and I too can let be, I thought, let the sun and moon and stars shine, let the trees grow and the waters flow, though they will anyway without my letting them. Still, I can command them in play, "He stood at the open window in the dark, took a deep breath and exhaled. The street lamps, like candles on a black cake, went out. He exhaled again and again and the stars began to vanish. . . . He pointed to the eastern sky. The sun began to rise."[7]

If "the sun also rises,"[8] yet the wonder of existence appears most clearly in the night sky, or so it seemed to me. Living in Texas in the hot summer, my mother and father let me, and later let my brother and sister too, sleep on cots in our backyard under the big night sky. I would lie on my back, looking up at the stars, thinking they were worlds like ours. "It is not *how* things are in the world that is mystical, but *that* it exists," Wittgenstein says.[9] That is what I was perceiving in the night sky, I believe, the mystical, *that* the world exists. The existence of God was linked in my mind to the wonder of existence. The wonder was not so much a proof as a sign of God's reality. To come to God from the wonder is an insight. It means no longer taking for granted what is most taken for granted, the existence of things, and when that is no longer taken for granted, God's presence appears.

And I felt the wonder of my own existence, again like the boy in *Dandelion Wine*, when he exclaimed "I'm alive!" He was wrestling with his brother, rolling over and over in the woods, when he stopped, dazed with the wonder of it. His brother said, "Are you all right?" But he gave a great soundless shout inside himself, "I'm alive! I'm really alive!"[10] And I, as I lay, looking up at the stars, thinking they were suns like ours, perhaps with inhabited worlds like ours circling around them, I felt the vastness of the universe and the wonder of my own being, that I am alive, that I am here and not there, that it is now and not then. My own presence to myself is linked to God's presence to me, as if to say God has chosen me to exist. So I am, I thought, and I am known and loved.

It was my grandfather who told me the names of the birds and the flowers and the trees and even the stars in the night sky. He was self-educated, having been to school only for the first few grades, but he was well read, as was my father, who was in school only through high school but read widely, carefully annotating our set of the Harvard Classics. I acquired a love of learning from the two of them, my father and my mother's father, and an idea of learning by reading. Although I had a much more extensive education afterwards in school than they did, I always felt that I was learning what I learned like them by my own reading.

I acquired from my father and my mother's father the idea of reading to learn, and I acquired from my mother, who already had a college education and was not trying to educate herself, the idea of reading for pleasure. I had a lamp over my bed, as did my mother and father, and we all read in bed at night. I was allowed to read as long as I wanted, but when I stopped reading I had to turn off the light and go to sleep. That was a considerable encouragement to reading. Also we used to go regularly to the public library and take books out. "Do you have something to read?" was a question my parents would ask, almost like "Did you have enough to eat?" If we were going somewhere and were going to have time on our hands, it was thought essential to have something to read. I don't know when I first learned to read, but it must have been early in my childhood, well before going to school.

I suppose I got the idea of being on a journey with God in time from walking with my grandfather and later from reading the Bible, "and Enoch walked with God: and he was not; for God took him."[11] We had a large Bible in the King James version that had belonged to George Scribner, my great grandfather on my father's side, who had studied to be a Presbyterian minister, I think at Princeton, but eloped with a woman, my great grandmother, against his father's wishes and went with her to California in the Gold Rush. I found this Bible fascinating, not just for the text but also for the appendices on the Rosetta Stone and the Behistun Inscription and other ancient matters connected with the Bible. We also had a set of Shakespeare's plays in separate small volumes. I used to look at these, but I didn't really read the plays until later in life. I used to browse also in our set of the Harvard Classics, but I actually read those things mostly in later life. Meanwhile I read things like the Oz stories by L. Frank Baum, the jungle stories of Frank Buck, and the adventures of Sherlock Holmes by Conan Doyle.

I still have a book my mother gave me on my tenth birthday, *The Life of Pasteur* by R. Vallery-Radot. The inscription reads, "To Scribner from Mother, Happy Birthday!—December 3, 1939." I was called Scribner in those early years, though I have been called John in these later years. I sometimes think the name Scribner is a destiny, for it means "writer." My mother would have loved to see me become a physician, and I was interested in reading Pasteur's life and similar things about the lives of physicians and the history of medicine. My father would have loved to see me become an architect, for he was a draftsman, though his middle name too was Scribner from his mother's last name and her father, George Scribner, and I used to spend many hours with him in "the shop," as he called it, the garage apartment behind our house where he would work on designs. I suppose being a draftsman was his way of being a scrivener as being a writer was mine, but I was not yet writing in these early years, unlike Jean Paul Sartre in his story of childhood, *The Words*, divided into two parts, Reading and Writing.

What then did I learn from my reading? I learned story, "our only boat for sailing on the river of time." Although I did not read *The Iliad* and *The Odyssey* until later, I did read stories of war and stories of adventure. So I learned of war and the journey. Also I did not ask the question until later in life, *Are we in a story?* and *What story are we in?* Yet all I was learning pointed to the story we are in and it was a story of war and the journey. The war in this first period of my life was the Second World War. What about the journey? That comes afterward, I suppose, as the *Odyssey* follows the *Iliad*. Reading was my way of participating in the war, as I was too young to fight, and reading was also my way of going on the journey. I was a young Don Quixote reading the romances of war and the journey as he read those of chivalry.

Am I in a story? That is the question that comes to me as I think of Don Quixote. For I not only read the stories of war and the journey but afterwards I actually set out on a journey, as he did, though mine was only to study, not to do chivalrous deeds, a journey to Austin, a journey to Notre Dame, a journey finally to Rome.

> Having come to this place
> I set out once again
> on the dark and marvelous way
> from where I began.[12]

To be in a story is to be on a "dark and marvelous way." It is dark, because there is the question Sam asks in Tolkien's trilogy, "I wonder what sort of a tale we've fallen into?" and Frodo's answer, "I wonder. But I don't know. And that is the way of a real tale. Take any one you're fond of. You may know, or guess, what kind of a tale it is, happy-ending or sad-ending, but the people in it don't know. And you don't want them to."[13] We often think we are in one story, my sister says, when actually we are in another. Her favorite example is Saint Benedict Joseph Labre. He thought he was in the story of a monk, and he went from monastery to monastery all over Europe, until he finally came to realize he was actually in the story of a pilgrim. My own story and my sister's may be similar to his, coming to realize we are on a journey with God in time.

Another question, and this is one my brother asks, is that of the truth of the story. An example he gives is from the story of Adam and Eve, a surface truth—the serpent saying "you will not die," and a deeper truth—God saying "you will die."[14] "Don't the great tales never end?" Sam goes on to ask. "No, they never end as tales," Frodo answers. "But the people in them come, and go when their part is ended. Our part will end later—or sooner."[15] My awareness of life opening up all the way to death did not come till later. A vivid awareness came when I was about thirty, but in this early period I was caught up rather in the thought that the great tales never end, that "we're in the same tale still!"

War and peace, that is the first of the great tales, and though I never read Tolstoy's *War and Peace* until later in life, I read much of the Second World War, especially of the sea battles, and I imagined myself becoming a sea captain. If I had actually become a sea captain, a friend told me in later life, I would be just the same as I am, I would look the same with my beard and I would tell stories as I do and as my grandfather did before me. But I couldn't imagine enduring the boredom of days at sea with nothing to occupy my mind. The only thing I can imagine doing that I would enjoy would be keeping the ship's log, like keeping a journal, something that I actually do and something that gives me a sense of being on a voyage or a journey. Perhaps that means that I actually belong in the other great tale, that of the journey rather than that of war.

Journey, the other of the great tales, is essentially a journey into the otherworld or a journey into the world of the other. I did not read the great epics of journey, Gilgamesh, Odysseus, Aeneas, Dante, until later in life, and so my early idea of the journey was from the Oz stories, a journey into an imaginary world. What is the point of such a journey? Adventure, also escape. But there is something deeper. There is a connection for me between travel and music, I have found in later life, so that music can take the place of travel in my life, as if in music I can go to faraway places and times, or even beyond place and time. "Song is the leap of mind in the eternal breaking out into sound."[16] What I am seeking in the journey, I think, is that leap of mind. I am seeking the eternal.

I find the eternal, I find that leap of mind in music, especially in composing. One of my earliest memories is waking up in a playpen and singing to awaken my mother and father. Music is something I learned from my mother, listening to her play the piano, playing especially the pieces she loved by the American composer Edward MacDowell, his Woodland Sketches such as "To a Wild Rose," one that I was able later to learn, but also more virtuoso pieces such as Second Hungarian Rhapsody by Liszt and Rhapsody in Blue by Gershwin. I began picking out melodies on the piano already when I was three years old. Then I took piano lessons in school, but I became inspired when I found a teacher, Sister Loyola, who took me off piano exercises and had me playing classical music. Later I learned clarinet from a really good jazz clarinetist and he and I used to play together on the local radio station. Piano and classical music was my real love, though, and I began to compose on the piano when I was a teenager, at first only dances and then, later, songs.

My schooling was nothing special until later. I went to kindergarten: the only incident I remember is another boy, named Chico, and I painting each other and coming home completely covered with gold paint. I went to a convent school for the first five grades, and I remember piano recitals there, one where I played Bach's Two-Part Invention #8, and I remember dances. My mother had the Quinn girls, friends of the family, teach me to dance at a very early age, and I learned from them, as I remember, the Texas Two Step. I didn't learn the clarinet until later, in public school, where I played in the school band.

Thinking of song as "the leap of mind in the eternal breaking out into sound,"[17] I find the presence of God especially in music and also in its opposite, silence. When I play the piano for a long time, I seem to be in another world, the other side of the brain perhaps, in contact with eternal things. There is a way of music then, and by contrast there is a way of words, a choice of ways for me, it has always seemed, though now in later life I see the ways coming together again into one way, as in Tolkien's words, "He used often to say there was only one Road; that it was like a great river: its springs were at every doorstep, and every path was its tributary."[18]

Story and song, therefore, are my way, words and music, the story of a journey and the song of God in time, and if there is a particular song it is a melody I thought of when I was still a teenager but in later life named *Ayasofya* in honor of the figure of Holy Wisdom.[19] "Most people die with their music still locked up inside of them," Benjamin Disraeli said.[20] My music, no longer locked up inside of me, is a song to Holy Wisdom, and it goes somehow with a journey with God in time. I think of the words of Knowledge to Everyman,

> Everyman,
> I will go with thee,
> and be thy guide,
> in thy most need
> to go by thy side.[21]

My grandfather was certainly a figure of wisdom for me with his stories and his naming of things as we walked together, and he wrote verse, something that I have been doing too in later life, and verse seems to combine the two elements of my way, words and music. My preparation for poetry in early life, though, were the two elements taken separately, words in my reading and music in my playing. My music was still locked up inside of me insofar as words and music had not yet come together for me. That is a fearful thing, to die with your music still locked up inside of you. On the other hand, is it enough to release your music, to express yourself in words and music before you die? I don't think I ever believed that would be enough for me. Instead, the content of my words and music has contained my hope, a journey with God like that of Enoch, who "walked with God, and he was not, for God took him."

A hurricane I was in when I was ten years old became for me an image of the journey in time. It was the summer of 1940, if I am not mistaken, and I was spending some weeks on the Gulf of Mexico with our next-door neighbors who had a place on Houston Bay. There was another boy there, ten years old, and several younger children including my sister. The adults had all gone into Houston and only we children were there when the hurricane struck, a large circular wind with a diameter of some miles. One edge of the hurricane struck in the afternoon and many trees fell. Then the quiet eye of the hurricane passed over us. Seeing the calm, we thought the storm was over, and someone said, "Let's go swimming!" So we ran out, the water having receded, and were swimming joyfully and shouting to one another. Then as it grew darker someone said, "It's getting scary!" So we all ran in again to shore and went into the old wooden house where we were staying. The electricity was out, and so we lit a lantern down in the bottom of the house—I remember the faces around the lantern—and we told ghost stories. The storm lasted through the night, and in the morning the adults came rushing back. We learned of the damage all around, but our old house stood and lost only a few shingles on the roof. The hurricane wind, according to the newspaper, had blown at 132 miles an hour.

In later years I saw in the moving storm with its quiet eye an image of the spiritual journey. You live in the quiet eye, for "we all have within us a center of stillness surrounded by silence,"[22] as Dag Hammarskjöld says, but you must keep moving to stay in the peace, for the storm has a path, and if you stand still the destructive edges of the storm will catch you.

There is a series of paintings by Thomas Cole (1801–1848) in the National Gallery in Washington, D.C., called *The Voyage of Life*. The first shows a little child with an angel behind him in a little boat coming out of a dark cave into the sunrise. The second shows a youth guiding the boat himself with the angel standing on shore and waving farewell and an imaginary or dreamlike city in the distance. The third shows a man in the boat, praying as he moves into the rapids, and a figure of light in heaven above and behind him. The fourth shows an old man in the boat, looking toward light in the darkened sky at sunset, and the figure of an angel, again near, and another angel in the distance along the path of light. As I write this, I see I have been talking about that first stage, the child in the boat with the angel, but I am in the fourth stage, the old man looking toward the light. And now I go on to the second, the youth looking to the ideal, and the third, the man praying in the crisis of his life.

Thomas Cole, *The Voyage of Life: Childhood*, 1842. Courtesy of the National Gallery of Art, Washington, D.C. Copyright © 2003. Ailsa Mellon Bruce Fund 1971.16.1.

A Quest of Happiness

> *The world of the happy man is a different one*
> *from that of the unhappy man.*
>
> —Wittgenstein

I just came across an autobiographical sketch I wrote many years ago, and I find that I divided my childhood in periods according to the ages of the world. The golden age was my preschool years (one to five); the silver age was my school years (six to ten); the bronze age was my public school years (ten to thirteen); and the iron age was my boarding school years (thirteen to fifteen). "The world of the happy man is a different one from that of the unhappy man,"[1] Wittgenstein says. My world was changing from a happy to an unhappy one. But I knew the happy world of my golden age, and that set me on a quest of happiness.

"We can know more than we can tell," Polanyi says, and that comes of dwelling in the particulars of what we know, dwelling in "the particulars of my life," as Shakespeare calls them,[2] and it is there in the particulars that there is sorrow and unhappiness. "All happy families resemble one another," as Tolstoy says in the opening sentence of *Anna Karenina*, "but each unhappy family is unhappy in its own way."[3] My mother's sorrow was the loss of her mother and father, her mother in a car accident and her father a year after the accident. My father's sorrow was the mental illness of his mother. Their sorrow came through to me as unhappiness and passed on through me to my sister and my brother, who were younger.

I found myself then on a quest of happiness. My mother and father, perceiving my unhappiness, decided to send me away from home to boarding school. This then became my first sally in quest of happiness. We were living in Waco, though long before the troubles of 1993 that made it famous, and I went off to school in Austin, a hundred miles away. These were war years (1943–1945), and the school, Saint Edward's, was at that time a military school, and there was a high school, which I attended, as well as a university. So I wore a military uniform and soon became an officer because of my good grades in school, though I had no real competence in military matters. My experience there was of the journey rather than of the war. It was an experience of encounter with other persons, some of them from Mexico, such as my roommate, and an experience of loneliness of being on my own and having my own life.

My first real journey away from home, my first sally in quest of happiness, therefore, was an odyssey, a journey into wonderland and in the summers a return to homeland. The wonderland part, away from home, was like the original *Odyssey*, a series of encounters with dread and fascination, with the dread and fascination of the mystery of life, a mystery that "shows itself and at the same time withdraws"[4] in human relations, and I found myself fleeing from life, not going anymore to dances, asking my teachers the question "Is it an obligation to get married?" For I tacitly believed marriage to be unhappy, like the marriage of my mother and father, and I was fleeing from un-happiness as I was fleeing from home. The fascination was there too, but the dread was much stronger.

Returning home in the summers then was not returning to hap-piness or winning through to happiness as in the original *Odyssey* but confronting unhappiness. Still, it had something in it of the happy return to family and the familiar. All the same, I did not identify hap-piness with home, as in the original *Odyssey,* but tacitly I took it to be in the journey itself, as I later found in *A Modern Sequel to the Odyssey* by Nikos Kazantzakis, where Odysseus cannot stay home but goes on again to journey, where it is said, "your voyages have been your native land,"[5] and I see that is still true for me, taking my life as a journey with God in time. And my later and more positive concept of mar-riage too has been that of a journey together, where two persons set out on an adventure together, side by side.

My second sally in pursuit of happiness was a spiritual quest, and it followed closely on my journey away from home. It was a study of the persons I was meeting, a study especially of their faces to see if they were happy and to learn from them the secret of happiness. This was the beginning for me of something that I have been doing ever since, *passing over* as I have called it in later years, entering into other lives and times, and then *coming back* with new insight to my own life and times. Passing over to fellow students was passing over to fellow seekers, not finders; passing over to teachers, on the other hand, was passing over to finders, or so I hoped. The teachers were priests and brothers of Holy Cross, and so I hoped to learn from those who were happy the secret of their happiness.

What was the secret of their happiness? There was a book I found around this time, the spiritual classic called *The Imitation of Christ.* The striking thing for me was the opening sentence, "One who follows me will not walk in darkness,"[6] a quotation from the Gospel of John. I thought I saw in that sentence the secret of happiness of the priests and brothers. They were following Christ and so they were not walking in darkness. To walk in darkness, as I understood it, was to walk in unhappiness. The secret of happiness was to follow Christ.

Following Christ, as I understood it from the lives of my teachers, meant living a simple life. Walking in darkness, on the other hand, meant living a complex life. I remember studying Latin at the time and learning the word *impedimenta*, which meant the supplies that an army had to bring along and that impeded its speedy movement. A simple life meant a life relatively free of *impedimenta*. A complex life meant a life fraught with them. Passing over into the lives of my teachers, I found this simplicity, or so it seemed to me, but I found also some dissatisfaction, especially in one teacher that I got to know well. He was dissatisfied not with the life of simplicity, it seemed, but with being at Saint Edward's. I saw in him then not a finder of happiness but, like myself, a seeker.

Coming back to myself and my own life, I found myself ready to set out on my own spiritual adventure. I wondered if I had a vocation to the priesthood. I read somewhere that the priest is essentially a man for others, and I knew I was not that, caught up as I was in my own quest of happiness. Yet I thought maybe I could grow into it someday: as I became a happy man I could become a man for others. Meanwhile I read the lives of the saints and I read the *Spiritual Exercises* of Saint Ignatius. I was "dreaming on things to come," as Shakespeare says,[7] and the hill on which Saint Edward's is built, overlooking Austin, became my hill of dreams.

My third sally in quest of happiness then was to go to Notre Dame to join the priests of Holy Cross. It was not until I got there, I believe, that I read the two lives of saints that meant the most to me, the life of

Saint Francis of Assisi and that of Saint Thomas Aquinas by G. K. Chesterton. There was a passage in the life of Saint Francis about him being in love with God.[8] That was inspiring for me. I wanted to be in love with God. And there was a chapter in the life of Saint Thomas called "The Real Life of Saint Thomas"[9] about his spiritual life. That too was inspiring for me. I wanted to have "a real life," a spiritual life, a life of prayer and contemplation. As it was, I had only the desire to be in love with God, only the desire to have a spiritual life. Later I read treatises by Saint Francis de Sales and got from him the idea that wanting to believe is believing, wanting to hope is hoping, wanting to love is loving.

I was trying already at this early date to combine the love of God and the love of learning. I wrote a sentence outline of Newman's essay on "Knowledge and Learning"[10] in this last year of high school in the seminary at Notre Dame. This was my first venture into philosophical thinking. Newman's distinction between knowledge and learning was a revelation for me, for I had acquired a love of learning from my grandfather and my father and also an ideal of self-education by reading, but now at the age of sixteen I found a new and higher goal, that of knowledge. To be learned was to be well read and well informed, but to have knowledge was to have insight and understanding. It was to have vision. It was for me the beginning of a quest of vision. My quest of happiness was changing into a quest of wisdom.

My second year after coming to Notre Dame was a year away, a year of novitiate, a year really of monastic life. One thing I was trying to learn was to practice the presence of God. I remember one day when we were working in silence, tying up vines in the dead of winter. It was so cold that when you took off your gloves to tie a vine on the strings between posts your fingers would become numb and you had to put your gloves on quickly again and clap your hands together to get the blood circulating in them. Well, in the silence I was trying to practice the presence of God, but I was drawing a blank. No presence. All I experienced was my own striving, my own efforts to practice the presence. It was like trying to prove the existence of God. "When I let the proof go," Kierkegaard says, "the existence is there."[11]

After the year of novitiate I began college at Notre Dame. At that time there was a blind music master there, Carl Mathes, who had studied with Béla Bartók. He took an interest in me and wanted to teach me keyboard harmony. I was very excited to work with him, but I was having trouble with a mathematics course and I decided fatefully that I had no time for music. In later years when I returned to music I wrote,

> Once the way of music
> was my way,
> and my blind master wished
> to teach me how to listen
> as the blind do
> and to improvise,
> but now the way of words
> has been my way
> into the dark with love,
> and now I listen like the blind,
> and hearing,
> I compose.[12]

To say "Once the way of music was my way" may be an overstatement. I used to compose as a teenager, and my most complete piece was a dance that I named Elf Dance at the time and many years later used in a song and dance cycle called The Church of the Poor Devil, and the dance itself I renamed then The Dance of the Spirits. When I was in the seminary at Notre Dame, I composed a Mass, that is, a Kyrie, a Sanctus, and an Agnus Dei. I later used the melody for the Kyrie in a song cycle called Ayasofya. These were all written in the forties and then revived in the nineties when I returned to music—fifty years later! Meanwhile, in the forties, when I was beginning college, I was seriously considering the possibility of becoming a priest composer, with such figures as Tomas Luis de Vittoria and Antonio Vivaldi as models.

My shifting from the way of music to the way of words went with the feeling of being more at home in the realm of words than in the realm of music. I have often thought words are my right hand and music is my left, and I am right-handed, so words have always been primary for me. If music is linked to the right brain and words to the left brain, being right-handed as I am connects with the left brain, though my left hand is very useful from playing the bass part on the piano while the right hand plays the treble. Later in life, much later, just before I returned to music, I had a dream in which the words came, "Explore the realm of music!" Words have always been the known world for me and music the unknown world, thus a world to be explored. I have a confidence with words, it seems, that I lack with music.

It is true, "we can know more than we can tell," as I keep quoting from Michael Polanyi, and so we can know more than we can tell in words, and what we know that we cannot tell we can express in music. I have always known this, it seems, and so I have always known that words without music are not enough, and so too is music without words, "songs without words"[13] as Mendelssohn called them. So in my quest of vision, my quest of wisdom, I have looked to words for vision, for wisdom, always knowing that vision is to be found, wisdom is to be found ultimately in words with music. Wisdom ultimately is what Vico calls "poetic wisdom."[14]

Following the way of words, I came during the summer after my second year in college to read the *Summa Theologiae* of Saint Thomas. It took the whole summer to read, and I was not reading everything, only the body of each article, skipping the objections and the answers to objections. Reading it article by article, I was getting the vision of things, how everything comes from God, how human beings return to God, and how Christ is the way. As I read I became more and more peaceful and serene. I was finding the happiness I had so long been seeking, finding it in a most unexpected place, reading a book, entering into a vision. Once I had gone through the *Summa* I wanted to do it again and again, and so I continued on year after year, reading it over and over and feeling again and again the peace and serenity of the vision of everything coming from God and returning again to God.

I found that if I was emotionally upset, I would become peaceful and serene after a few days into reading the *Summa*. I took it that the mind of Saint Thomas was an intuitive rather than a discursive mind, though he cast his writing into discursive form with arguments and counter arguments to articulate his vision for students. My interest, though, was in the vision itself, a vision similar to that of Saint Augustine in his *Confessions:* "the story of the soul wandering away from God and then in torment and tears finding its way home through conversion is also the story of the entire created order."[15] I found the peace and serenity then also in reading the *Confessions,* though I found there also the "torment and tears" which I didn't find in the *Summa*. Still, my own experience was essentially a peace of mind, as I was living in my mind like Thomas rather than living in my heart like Augustine.

I suppose it is possible to love God "with all your mind," as I did, without knowing yet how to love God "with all your heart, and with all your soul, and with all your might." I should not assume that Saint Thomas loved God only with all his mind like this, though that is the love I acquired from him along with a great peace of mind. Still, it is from Saint Augustine that I could more readily learn to love "with all your heart," but I had a lot of life to live before I could begin to learn that. Meanwhile the peace of mind that came to me from reading Saint Thomas was a real answer and a real fulfillment of my quest of happiness.

Now an ambition took hold of me, to do with modern thought what Saint Thomas had done with ancient thought. I began to read Kant and I saw in his *Critique of Pure Reason* something corresponding to the first part of the *Summa* about everything coming from God, and I saw in his *Critique of Practical Reason* something corresponding to the second part of the *Summa* about human beings returning to God. But then I realized Kant was working from Newton's science, taking space and time to be the human sensorium, where Newton had taken them to be the divine sensorium. I realized I would have to work instead from Einstein's science, taking space and time to be the sensorium of the moving observer. I was fascinated with the way Einstein was able from the principle of relativity to derive formulas for the relation of matter and energy and formulas for the motion of the planets. I began to collect principles like this to form the basis of a kind of *Summa*.

Somewhere in there I came upon an idea that I have entertained ever since then, that matter is a dimension like time and like the three dimensions of space. This was a seminal idea. Later I wrote to Erwin Schrödinger, the physicist who devised the wave equation in Quantum Theory. I asked him if he thought the idea was viable, and I got a one-sentence reply, "Matter is not a dimension."[16] Still, I thought of matter as a dimension, and at the other end of things there was God, and I knew "God is spirit"[17] from the Gospel of John, and I thought of God as acting spiritually, illumining the mind and kindling the heart. If matter is a dimension, I asked myself, then what is in the dimensions? Events, I supposed. "The universe is a series of leaping sparks—everything else is interpretation,"[18] it has been said. My interpretation was events. The world is a series of events, a history that comes from God and goes to God. My vision then was like that in the *Summa*, everything coming from God and returning to God, but instead of substances it was of events.

I saw the poetic counterpart of the *Summa* in Dante's *Divine Comedy*, and I even contemplated some kind of musical setting for it. I wasn't able yet to work this out, though, for Dante begins "lost in a dark wood"[19] and ends caught up in "the love that moves the sun and the other stars,"[20] but I knew as yet only how to love God "with all your mind," and I had a long journey to go to learn how to love "with all your heart, and with all your soul, and with all your might." If wisdom is "poetic wisdom," as Vico says, I was not yet capable of it, though my calling was clearly to wisdom rather than to science. I had a glimpse of wisdom of the heart, though, in a seminar I took on ethics with Jacques Maritain, when he said to my astonishment "God is vulnerable."[21]

I had my first experience teaching around this time. My classmates used to have me give a review session in philosophy each semester before the final exams. What I would do is outline the course as I understood it. This was my first teaching experience apart from a catechism class I taught to Mexican boys in the summer before my novitiate year. The outlining went with all the other writing I did in those years, starting with the sentence outline I had made of Newman's essay on Knowledge and Learning. I made outlines especially of the *Summa* from my repeated readings, and I made outlines or sketches of my own ideas for a kind of *Summa,* trying to do with modern thought what Saint Thomas had done with classical thought, and I made outlines of my ideas in science. Yet in all this I was reaching for vision and for wisdom.

As I went on I seemed to find thought diverging instead of converging upon a peaceful vision. Meanwhile I learned I was going to be sent to Rome to study theology after graduating from Notre Dame, and I thought I might find in my studies there in Rome the convergence of vision that I was seeking. In the second of his paintings on *The Voyage of Life* Thomas Cole has the youth in the storyboat alone, looking to a vision, while the angel waves farewell from shore. I too was in my storyboat alone at this point, looking for a vision, not yet fully aware of my journey in time and of God my companion on the way.

Thomas Cole, *The Voyage of Life: Youth*, 1842. Courtesy of the National Gallery of Art, Washington, D.C. Copyright © 2003. Ailsa Mellon Bruce Fund 1971.16.2.

An Italian Journey

Et in Arcadia ego.

—epigraph of Goethe's
Italian Journey

Going to Rome, I found my vision changing with the image of the city to something like Saint Augustine's vision of *The City of God*, "For here have we no continuing city, but we seek one to come."[1] It was close to my later vision of a journey with God in time, but it was nevertheless an image of a city rather than an image of traveling. All the same, my time in Italy was a time of traveling, the voyage over and back, the journeys to and from Rome, the summers in the Alps.

"It was at Rome, on the 15th of October, 1764," Edward Gibbon writes, "as I sat musing amidst the ruins of the Capitol, while the barefoot friars were singing vespers in the Temple of Jupiter, that the idea of writing the decline and fall of the city first started to my mind."[2] My own experience of Rome too was an encounter with the past, though my mind toward the past was uncritical by comparison with Gibbon's, who saw Christianity as the cause of the decline and fall of the Roman Empire. *Et in Arcadia ego,* "and I was in Arcadia,"[3] Goethe's epigraph to his *Italian Journey,* a tomb inscription often depicted in classical paintings, was true for me too: I was in Arcadia. I was enjoying my encounter with ancient Rome, with Renaissance Rome, with modern Rome, and I felt I was learning something from each of them. I was acquiring a vision, though my mind was uncritical too by comparison with Goethe's as he was shaking off a romantic for a classical vision.

My own uncritical approach to Rome left me open to religious elements in art and culture, open to the idea I found at that time in the writings of Christopher Dawson, "religion is the soul of culture."[4] I was ready for an encounter with the soul of the ancient city, with the soul of the Renaissance, and with the modern soul. I was confident, from the peacefulness I found reading the *Summa,* that I would be able to find peace and serenity again, and that I would discover in this the guiding vision that I was seeking.

Our voyage across the Atlantic was my first real sea voyage. Now my childhood ambition to be a sea captain was tested with the boredom of days at sea. Still, there was excitement, and the voyage became for me an image of life as a voyage of discovery. Our ship was the *Constitution* of American Export Lines, and we took the southern route from New York via the Azores to Cadiz, then on to Gibraltar, then on in sight of Tangier and Mount Atlas across the Mediterranean and past Sicily to Naples. There were four of us traveling together, two Americans and two French Canadians, and we were met at Naples and went by ground car to Rome. Our arrival at last in Rome seemed to have a spiritual significance, as if to say our "life's uncertain voyage"[5] ends, its uncertainty resolved, with our arrival in the Eternal City.

Our arrival was for me the beginning of a process of passing over, first of all to the ancient city of Rome, entering into the journey Virgil describes in the *Aeneid,* which I had read by this time, especially book VI, describing the journey of Aeneas into the otherworld, the land of the dead but also of the unborn. The illustrious men and women of ancient Rome, unborn for Aeneas, were the dead for me. I was seeing them as immortal souls, not just as figures living in our memory of them, and the Virgil I knew was the Virgil who led Dante through the otherworld. So the ruins too of the Forum and the Palatine I was seeing with an eye like Augustine's rather than an eye like Gibbon's, "For here have we no continuing city, but we seek one to come." Immortality was not a continuity on earth but was immortality of the soul.

Thus my journey among the ruins was a kind of journey into the otherworld, the Capitoline Hill, the Forum and the Palatine, the Forum of Trajan and the other Fori Imperiali, the Colosseum, the Circus Maximus, the Baths of Caracalla. That feeling of otherworld was enhanced by many of the ruins being underground. The detritus of the centuries has piled up and the ancient city is partly below earth. There is the underground palace of Nero, and there is the temple of Mithras under the church of San Clemente, and there are the catacombs and the many tombs with the inscription DMS, *dis manibus sacrum,* "sacred to the gods below." There were the gods above and the gods below, the gods of the living and the gods of the dead. These gods of the dead, the Manes, were all that remained of the old gods after the decline and fall of the Roman Empire. Or so it seemed to me wandering among the ruins.

"Easy is the descent into the netherworld," *Facilis descensus Averno,* Aeneas is told,[6] but coming back is the thing that is difficult. Coming back from the Roman netherworld, I was coming back to present-day Rome and my theological studies. We were living on Via Aldrovandi, on the edge of the Villa Borghese, right across from the zoo, the Giardino Zoologico, and so we would walk through the Villa Borghese every morning on our way to school. That first year all four of us were going to the Angelico, the Dominican school of theology in Rome. I wanted to go there because of my love of reading the *Summa* and because I knew their theology was entirely based on it. My ambition to do with modern thought what Saint Thomas did with classical thought made me restless, though, with the closure of theology on the *Summa,* and so I decided to transfer after that first year to the Gregorian, the Jesuit school of theology in Rome.

"We are too late for the gods and too early for Being,"[7] Heidegger says. I was feeling too late for the gods, as I wandered among the ruins, and too early for Being, as I sought for a way of bringing faith to modern thought. The summer following that first year we stayed at Bressanone in the Dolomites, and we went on a ten-day hike in the Alps, going through the Brenner Pass. Meanwhile I was reading Saint Thomas *On Being and Essence,* seeing in that short and early work of his the essence of his thought and casting about for something similar in my own project of bringing faith to modern thought, feeling indeed "too early for Being."

Our return to Rome from our summer in the Dolomites was for me a return to the process of passing over, now to Renaissance Rome as well as to ancient Rome. After saying we are "too early for Being," Heidegger goes on to say we human beings are "Being's poem, just begun." The human body, it seems, is the poem of the Renaissance. The method of Leonardo, the method of Michelangelo, as I understand it now, is one of consciously dwelling in the particulars of what we know of the human body. My father was a draftsman, and watching him at work on design, I learned of attention to particulars. I have often thought my method of writing, a paragraph in a day, is just like his method of drawing. Dwelling in the particulars of what we know of the human body, like Leonardo and Michelangelo, goes with dwelling in the particulars of what we know of the physical universe, like Galileo. Passing over into this method, I was seeing the human body in terms of the universe and seeing the universe in terms of the human body.

Seeing the Sistine Chapel, for instance, I saw Michelangelo dwelling in the particulars of the human body, envisioning the beginning and the ending of all things in terms of the human body. The beginning is there in the body of Adam and the body of Eve in the creation scenes on the ceiling, and the ending is there in the body of Christ and the body of Mary and the bodies of the saved and the damned in the Last Judgment scene. "For until you have seen the Sistine Chapel, you can have no adequate conception of what man is capable of accomplishing,"[8] Goethe says in his *Italian Journey*. What are we capable of accomplishing? What am I capable of accomplishing? That was the question for me at this time.

Coming back from the Renaissance to my theological studies, I was attracted to the work of Nicolas Cusanus (we had been in his town of Chiusa in the summer), his *Learned Ignorance*, a Renaissance theology and a model of what I wanted to do in theology. Meanwhile I was encountering a tendency in my theology courses to condemn all that was modern, and there was the Oath against Modernism that I had to take at each step along the way to the priesthood and the degree in theology. What was condemned, it seems, was an evolutionary and symbolic view of dogma. I took the Oath again and again over the years until I came to a point where I realized I could not take it anymore. Then I asked the Superior of our house, Father Edward Heston, if I might recite the Nicene Creed instead of the Oath, and he said "Sure," as though there were no problem. That was later on, I believe, when I was up to receive the doctorate in theology (in 1957). As it turned out, reciting the Creed instead of the Oath became the norm ten years later (in 1967).

Anyway, that summer (1953) we stayed at Lake Como and went hiking again in the Alps. Goethe came to Lake Como on his way back from his Italian journey. For him it was coming back from art to nature. "I am buying myself a hammer and will strike rocks to drive away the bitterness of death," he wrote in a letter. "Thus does human nature cast about for help when there is no help left."[9] For me too it was coming back from civilization to nature. I don't know if I was striking rocks to drive away the bitterness of death or casting about for help when there was no help left, but I needed to get away from theology somehow, to find a new approach to it. I remember vividly coming down from the Alps by way of the Stelvio Pass, down, down, down into Italy.

Returning again to Rome, I was passing over now to modern Rome and modern Catholicism in its crisis of renewal in the last days of Pope Pius XII. I read *Surnaturel* by Henri de Lubac and found there the outlines of a Catholicism reborn with roots in Saint Thomas on the natural desire for God and Saint Augustine on the heart restless until it rests in God. To bring the body and the soul together seemed to be the lesson of the Renaissance, the human body and the human soul, the body of the universe and the soul of the universe. To see the soul as "capable of God" (*anima est capax Dei*)[10] seemed to be the vision of *Surnaturel,* to see thought, even modern thought, pervaded by the natural desire to see God. Here were the beginnings of the vision I was looking for. I didn't know the work of Teilhard de Chardin at the time, his vision of all things evolving toward Omega, but the idea of a pervasive desire for God carried me in that direction.

Combining "the love of learning and the desire for God,"[11] I was living a life of study and prayer. In fact, study and prayer for me were one and the same, or the life of study and the life of prayer were one life. This came of reading the *Summa* again and again, taking a month or more each time to go through it, reading just for the vision of things. I would feel more and more peaceful and serene as I read on, and so for me this reading had the virtue of prayer. It was as though the intellectual life and the contemplative life were one and the same—it was learning to love God "with all your mind."[12]

Coming back to my theological studies, however, I began to read Protestant theologians in my search for a modern equivalent of the *Summa*. I read Karl Barth's lectures, *Dogmatics in Outline*, and learning that he was working on a *Summa*, the very thing I wanted to do, I thought of asking to study with him. I also read Rudolf Bultmann, his *Theology of the New Testament*, what he said about the message of Jesus, the theology of Saint Paul and the theology of Saint John. Here I found someone who brought faith to modern thought in the form of Heidegger's philosophy as Saint Thomas brought it to classical thought in the form of Aristotle's philosophy. This was my introduction, moreover, to Heidegger's *Being and Time*, to his thinking on human existence, but not yet to his later thinking on thinking.

We spent the summer (1954) in the Val d'Aosta in sight of the Matterhorn, the mountain the Italians call Cervino. It was a relief and a vacation just to see a mountain, and we could see it in all its majesty right there from the porch of the place where we were staying. The peace and serenity of that sight combined for me with the peace and serenity of my reading about everything coming from God and everything returning to God. That peaceful vision went with me as we traveled that summer, on to Mont Blanc, and over the Great Saint Bernard Pass, and down to Annecy and the world of Saint Francis de Sales, and over to Geneva and the world of John Calvin, and on to Lausanne.

Returning to Rome in August, we were moving from Via Aldrovandi and the Villa Borghese to Via Aurelia Antica and the Villa Doria Pamphili, and I was preparing for ordination to the priesthood. That vision I got from reading the *Summa*, of everything coming from God and returning to God, went with the idea of Christ as the way and culminated, like the unfinished *Summa*, in the real presence of Christ in the Eucharist. The priesthood, as I saw it, was the priesthood of the Eucharist, and its principal action was the celebration of Mass. I thought of the vision that came to Saint Thomas after writing on the Eucharist, Christ asking Thomas what reward he wished and Thomas answering "Nothing, Lord, but you."[13] I wanted to be able to say that too, as if God were saying to me, as in Solomon's dream, "Ask what I shall give you."[14]

It was the power and the glory that was given, as in Graham Greene's novel *The Power and the Glory*, "For thine is the kingdom and the power and the glory for ever,"[15] as the Lord's Prayer ends for Protestants, but the power and the glory is given to human beings in ordination, according to Catholics, even though priests are weak and sinful as in Greene's story. Our ordination to the priesthood took place in the Lateran Basilica on December 18, 1954, with Cardinal Micara presiding. My mother was there along with the mother of Joe Hoffman, one of my companions in ordination, and the two mothers traveled with us around Rome afterwards and on to Florence, and then went on themselves to Paris and to London, enjoying themselves thoroughly, while we settled into our new role as priests.

Around this time I first heard the lectures of Father Bernard Lonergan, who was to be my main teacher and the director of my doctoral dissertation. I read his articles on *Verbum*, the mental word in the teaching of Saint Thomas. I have come to see his thought as parallel to that of Michael Polanyi on personal knowledge, "we can know more than we can tell."[16] What we can tell, according to Lonergan, is articulated in the *mental word*; what we can know, on the other hand, is contained in the *insight* that gives rise to the mental word. I knew him in his earlier period when he was writing his book *Insight* and before he did his later and more systematic work *Method in Theology*. His advice to me, when I came to him with several alternative topics on Saint Thomas, was to write my dissertation on the idea of participation in the theology of Saint Thomas.

I spent the summer (1955) in France, working on my dissertation, living at L'Eau Vive, a retreat at Soisy about half an hour from Paris. I met some remarkable people there, including Jean Vanier, who was just beginning his work with the mentally retarded. I went to see Father L.-B. Geiger at the nearby Dominican monastery of Le Saulchoir, for he had written on the idea of participation in the philosophy of Saint Thomas. He was very kindly and encouraging of my project of writing on the same idea in the theology of Saint Thomas. In Plato's thought participation (*methexis*) is the relation of things to the transcendent ideas; in Saint Thomas then it is the relationship of things to God. If we can distinguish between philosophy and theology here, I suppose the philosophy of participation has to do with everything coming from God, while the theology of participation has to do with everything returning to God and Christ as the way.

Returning to Rome, I wrote a quick draft of my whole thesis, just spinning it out of my thoughts and relying on my familiarity with Saint Thomas from reading the *Summa*. Lonergan rejected this version of my thesis and told me to do it over again, this time examining all the texts where Saint Thomas speaks of participation. So I began a laborious process of writing down all the passages on participation and collecting them into piles according to subject, participation in divine happiness, in eternity, in divine light, in divine nature, and so on, trying to gain a specific insight into each kind of participation. I learned from all this a more inductive approach and one aiming at insight.

We are "too early for Being," Heidegger says, but I had to include the philosophy of participation in my theology of participation, and it is all about Being. There is Being and there are beings. Being is the wonder of existence, the wonder I felt as a child as I lay on summer nights looking up at the stars. Beings all participate in Being, each in their own way. "It is not *how* things are in the world that is the mystical, but *that* it exists,"[17] as Wittgenstein says. Being is that it exists, and so Being is "the mystical," but how things are in the world is participation, each thing having its own mode of participating in Being. According to Saint Thomas, moreover, God is Being by essence not just by participation. The whole wonder of existence thus is concentrated in God. Everything other than God participates in Being and has its own mode of participation.

Human beings too have an essence, the human essence or human nature, and so there is what we can be by nature and there is what we can be by participation. "Whereby are given unto us exceeding great and precious promises: that by these ye might be partakers of the divine nature."[18] This is the theology of participation. I was caught up in defining each instance, happiness as conscious well-being and our participation in divine happiness as our consciousness of God's well-being, eternity as timelessness rather than infinite time and our participation in eternity as our awareness of God's timelessness, grace as the illumining of the mind and the kindling of the heart by God's knowing and loving. My later sense of being on a journey with God in time, I believe, comes of this vision of sharing in God's own life.

Underlying all I found the idea that the soul is somehow all things (*anima est quodammodo omnia*) and the soul is capable of God (*anima est capax Dei*).[19] I connected this with Lonergan's idea of "the un-restricted desire to know"[20] and that with Saint Thomas's idea of a natural desire for the vision of God and Saint Augustine's idea that our heart is restless until it rests in God. The universal capacity for all things I saw as a capacity for God, and the unfulfilled capacity for God as a restless desire for God. This was the vision of things I had found also in *Surnaturel,* the human essence as the image of God, an unfulfilled capacity for God which we feel as a restless desire or yearning, what I now call *the heart's desire.*

That summer (1956) I took the Orient Express from Venice to Paris, and I went on to London and stayed at a parish called Saint Philomena's in the suburb of Pinner. I have never been a parish priest, and this was the only time in my life that I have ever really lived in a parish as a priest. It was a time of encounter with other persons, particularly with a beautiful young woman of French origin—I remember her wearing a mantilla. I must have met any number of women over the years, but this was the first time in a long time that my "eyes were opened,"[21] as in the story of Adam and Eve. Nothing happened, but it was the beginning of a new awareness for me. I had a very long way to go to learn about living in the heart. That summer, I believe it was, I went to visit my sister, who was a novice with the Sisters of Saint Mary at Namur in Belgium, near Waterloo, and that fall, it may have been, my brother came to visit me in Rome.

I had been living in my mind all these years, and the peace and serenity I found was in an intellectual vision of all things coming from God and all things returning to God and Christ as the way. I loved God, but it was with all my mind. I didn't know yet how to love "with all your heart, and with all your soul, and with all your might." My last days in Rome then were spent in concluding my work for the doctorate in theology. My thesis on participation was read and approved by

Father Lonergan and Father John Wright, and I gave the obligatory lecture before faculty, the *lectio coram*, on the doctrine of the Holy Trinity, and I gave the public defense of my thesis before a large audience at the Gregorian, all in Latin.

Then, after Easter, I went on to spend the spring and the summer in Paris before returning to America to teach. The Holy Cross Fathers had a house at that time in Paris on Rue Notre Dame des Champs near the Jardin des Tuilleries. I was the only English-speaking member of the house and so I was elected to be guest master and tour guide for all English-speaking visitors to the house. I soon worked out a tour of Paris, going around on the Metro, and ending with a tour of the Louvre, and concluding with the Mona Lisa of Leonardo. Each time, it seemed, or at least three times, I got engaged, always by a different person, in a discussion of the existence of God, in front of the Mona Lisa, smiling as if she knew some secret.

Then that summer (1957) I made the return voyage to America on the *Maasdam* of Holland-Amerika lines. We started from Rotterdam, went on to Southampton, stopped off at Cobh, where we could see how green Ireland is from the sea, then on across the North Atlantic, where we veered around to avoid an iceberg, and on to Halifax and then on to New York. I remember the ship having almost no roll but considerable pitch, and people getting seasick and the numbers on deck dwindling, and finally I got seasick myself as I was climbing stairs between decks. Arriving in America, I had been away so long, six years without coming back, I felt alien. I was eager, though, to begin my teaching, and to share the vision I had gained.

To Choose/to Discover the Way

"My heart speaks clearly at last."
—J. R. R. Tolkien

When life opens up before you all the way to death, then you have to choose or else to discover your way in life. That is what was happening for me when I returned to America and began my teaching at Notre Dame. Life opened up before me all the way to death—I was twenty-seven when I began teaching, and by the time I was twenty-nine or thirty I had become aware that my youth was passing and that some-day I would die. At the same time, as I started teaching, I had read Sartre and thought we simply choose our way in life, we "choose our essence" or our "existence precedes essence,"[1] as he says, but I soon learned, from teaching, from reading, from counseling others who were finding their way, that we do not simply choose, we discover our way in life.

I learned first from teaching. For Sartre's position, that we simply choose our way, was based on the assumption that there is no God. Starting from the contrary position, that God exists, I had to think things out again from the beginning: if there is a God, then there is a way, and if there is a way, then we discover it, we don't simply choose it. "Faith seeking understanding" (*fides quaerens intellectum*),[2] that is what I took theology to be, a faith in God that seeks an understanding of life. Students were coming to me with faith, I could see, and they were seeking an understanding of life. When I first began teaching in the late fifties, faith was taken for granted, but then in the sixties it was no longer taken for granted, and it became necessary, so I thought, to consider atheism, like that of Sartre and Camus and Nietzsche, in order to go from childhood belief to a personal appropriation of faith, to help students take what Kierkegaard called "the leap of faith."[3]

I learned also from reading, especially from reading Tolkien. It is true, I did not discover Tolkien until the sixties, when my sister recommended reading Tolkien's trilogy, *The Lord of the Rings*. There I found scattered through the story the four little sentences that I took to be four spiritual truths:

> Things are meant;
> there are signs;
> the heart speaks;
> there is a way.[4]

As I understood it, "Things are meant" are the things that enter a life and belong to a life, the situations and the persons of the life, and to say they are *meant* is to say they do belong and there is more than chance in these encounters, though what the purpose may be has still to be discovered; "there are signs" are indicators, positive signs such as encouraging results or encouraging words from others, negative signs such as uneasiness and even sickness with paths that are not right for us; "the heart speaks" is a harmony of thought and feeling, an inner peace and serenity with paths that are right, something to wait for rather than making an arbitrary decision; and "there is a way" is the existence of a path even when it seems there is no way, a path that may already be laid before our feet, though we do not yet discern it.

I learned finally from counseling others who were finding their way. I could see they were not simply choosing their work in life and their partner in life but they were discovering their own desires and abilities, discovering a relationship with another person. They were choosing, it is true, but their choice was a consent to something they had discovered. I realized this is how I had found my own way in life, not simply choosing among equal and opposite alternatives but discovering my way in life, discovering what I later called "the road of the heart's desire."

It was in writing my first book, *The City of the Gods*, as life opened up before me all the way to death, that I began to live in my heart. I did not set out to write about life opening to death, though that was happening for me at this time. I had the title, *The City of the Gods*,[5] but my intention was to write on the political theology of the ancient city. I had been reading Arnold Toynbee and Eric Voegelin and I thought to write a theological vision of history, like Saint Augustine's *City of God*, and I received a Rockefeller grant to do a year of research and writing at Princeton. After I got there in Princeton, though, I could not get started with the writing and I spent my time reading. I was reading the classics, but my feelings were all about my youth passing and my life opening up before me to death.

So I read also the epic of Gilgamesh, for it is all about becoming aware of your mortality and going in quest of eternal life, and I read

Heidegger's essay on death in *Being and Time,* where he talks about living toward death and becoming free toward death. Then it occurred to me that Gilgamesh and Heidegger are at either end of history and that a line going from the one to the other passes through all the historic answers to death. I thought then of changing the subject of my book and writing about the answers to death over the ages, including the ancient city but going on to the present day. With that I became excited and began to write. I did a quick draft of the whole book, but then, as with my dissertation, I went back and started a slow process of careful writing, one step at a time, delving into each historic answer to death.

I came to the idea that each human society, each culture or civilization, had its own answer to death, and this answer was the fundamental myth of the society, for instance our own society with its myth of autonomy, of living toward death, as Heidegger says, and becoming free toward death ("You accept death, and then you're free!" as a student said to me some years later), or medieval society with its myth of hierarchy, of lords spiritual and lords temporal, of the king with his two bodies, a body natural that dies and a body politic that never dies, or the society of the Roman Empire with its sense of a universal human nature and a gamut of human experience that could be run before death, or the ancient republics with their ideal of doing immortal deeds and living on in human memory, or the ancient kingdoms with their sense of the relation between the living and the dead, that the king must live and the king must die.

"If I must die someday, what can I do to fulfill my desire to live?" That is how I formulated the question of death, but that was in the end, after I had written most of the book and was writing the conclusion and the preface. I started with Gilgamesh and his quest of eternal life. For him the question was "Must I die someday?" Then I went on to ancient Egypt where the question was about the relation of the living to the dead and the land of the living to the land of the dead. Then I went to the *Iliad* and the *Odyssey*, where I found an acceptance of death and of mortal existence, and then on to classical ideas of living on in the memory of others and of running the gamut of experience in life, and on to ideas of immortality of the soul in Plato's *Dialogues* and Virgil's *Aeneid*. At that point in time I saw the coming of Christ, but I didn't get the full impact of his resurrection until I came to writing the conclusion. Meanwhile I went on to later ideas such as "the king never dies," in the middle ages, and to modern ideas like that of Heidegger on living toward death and becoming free toward death.

It was at the end, writing the conclusion, that I found the answer to death in Christ's "words of eternal life"[6] in the Gospel of John. "I am the resurrection and the life," he says; "one who believes in me, though dead, shall live; and whoever lives and believes in me shall never die."[7] These words spoke to my heart, and though I had heard them many times before, they had never spoken to me as they did now, after I had become conscious of my own mortality and gone on a kind of Gilgamesh quest of eternal life. Where Gilgamesh journeyed toward the sunrise, I journeyed in time, going through human history, looking for answers to death. And I found Christ's "words of eternal life" more impressive and convincing than the words about living in memory or running the gamut of experience or becoming free toward death. It was as if I had encountered Christ risen from the dead.

"Do not seek death. Death will find you. But seek the road which makes death a fullfilment,"[8] Dag Hammarskjöld writes in his diary, *Markings*. Which is the road that makes death a fulfillment for me? That became the question for me after *The City of the Gods*, my Gilgamesh quest of eternal life. I thought at first that individuals would simply be instances of the answer to death in society, but then I saw how personal memory of the past meant a similarly personal anticipation of the future. Saint Augustine's *Confessions*, I saw, were a search for God in time and memory. So just as my first book corresponded to his *City of God*, I wanted my second to correspond to his *Confessions*, not an autobiography like this one but a study of autobiographies including that of Augustine himself.

To be sure, to understand the autobiographies of others I had to sketch out my own, but I didn't include this in the book, and reading it over now, I see I was trying to understand my own life in terms of Augustine's. I saw him as a prototype of the modern person who is essentially lonely, who has lost all sense of mediation, of spiritual and temporal mediators, that belonged to the hierarchical society of the middle ages, and who lives in the alienation and autonomy that belong to our own lives and times. Augustine, though, seemed to provide an answer to the loneliness with his sense of the presence of God in time and memory.

"May I know me! May I know thee!"[9] Saint Augustine's prayer in his *Soliloquies*, became my prayer. I could see how he progressed over a period of ten years from that brief prayer to the sustained prayer of his *Confessions*. Here I am writing an autobiography at the end of my life, and I am still unable to sustain prayer as he did in his, but I can enter into that brief surge of the spirit, "May I know me! May I know thee!" It is said in *The Cloud of Unknowing*, "Short prayer penetrates heaven."[10] That has to be my hope. Sustained prayer, like that of Augustine in his *Confessions*, means living in the standpoint of the person before God. There is the standpoint of the person before others, as in an *Apologia pro Vita Sua* like Newman's, and there is the standpoint of the person before self, as in Augustine's *Soliloquies*, and there is finally the standpoint of the person before God, as in his *Confessions*.

Writing this autobiography, I am before others and before myself, but in short prayer that penetrates heaven, I hope, I am before God.

"May I know me!" Bringing time to mind, I found, is the key to knowing yourself. There is the immediate person who lives in the moment like a little child, and then there is the existential person who is aware of having a past and a future and is concerned about which way to go in life, and then there is the historic person who is aware of having a life and times and is concerned about relating to life and to the times. *Passing over* to other lives and times became a conscious project for me in writing this second book, and *coming back* with new insight to my own life and times. All human beings could be seen as standing in a great circle, I thought, call it the human circle, each one located on the circle by the particulars of their life, and from each point on the circumference a radial path could be traced to the center, a particular way to the heart's desire. At the center of everything, I thought, is the human heart's desire, as in Augustine's words, "our heart is restless until it rest in thee."[11]

"May I know thee!" Thinking back, the kind of thinking you do in an autobiography, can become thinking back to the beginning, and that is what it became for Saint Augustine in his *Confessions,* and so in the last books or chapters he speaks of memory and time and the beginning of time. Following his lead, I named my book *A Search for God in Time and Memory.*[12] In this book, I realized, I was thinking back to my beginning just as in my first book I was thinking forward to my end. Thinking back, I was becoming contemporary with the beginning of time, I thought, like Kierkegaard becoming contemporary with Christ.[13] Somehow all these things are one, becoming contemporary with the beginning, becoming contemporary with the end, and becoming contemporary with Christ. Knowing God means coming to the edges of time, I found. It means coming to know the eternal in us.

"My life is a journey in time and God is my companion on the way," I wrote in my first diary around this time in 1968, when I was completing this second book and was about to set out on a solitary journey through Latin America. "My life is a journey in time" is an answer to the prayer "May I know me!" and "God is my companion on the way" is an answer to "May I know thee!" I had a way to go, nevertheless, to learn how real these things are, for I added in my diary "I sometimes wish that it were more literally a journey, from one place and time to another, and that I had a human companion, visible and tangible." I had still to learn how real the journey is in time and how real God's companionship can be. "I only know now how real these things are," Jung's remark about the great symbols after his hospital experience, is true for me too after my own hospital experience, I only know now how real these things are. All the same, the journey in time and God-with-us became already then the guiding symbols of my life.

From this point on I have diaries to go on, showing what I was thinking at the time, sometimes in contrast to what I am thinking now in retrospect. One thing I was thinking then, as I set out on my journey through Latin America, was that I might not come back. "It has occurred to me that I might not come back from this journey alive," I wrote in my diary. "There are many chances and risks involved. Many of the things which have happened to me lately have the ring of a valediction." What actually happened is that my mother died, the day after I returned from Latin America. That journey, then, was an end and a beginning for me. Your mother and your father stand between you and death, and you don't realize until they are gone how they shielded you from death.

" In my beginning is my end," T. S. Eliot writes in his *Four Quartets*, and "In my end is my beginning."[14] In *The City of the Gods* I was thinking forward to my end, and in *A Search for God in Time and*

Memory I was thinking back to my beginning. Now as I journeyed through Latin America, stopping a few days at Rio, then at Buenos Aires, on my way to give conferences to the Holy Cross priests in Santiago, I was thinking of what I should do next in my writing. It was on my way back, stopping in Peru to go to Cuzco and Macchu Picchu, watching the sunset and then afterwards the sunrise over the ancient city of refuge at Macchu Picchu, that I began to find a new inspiration. "Not to be afraid of Freud and Marx," I told myself, Freud saying religion is wishful belief and Marx saying it is the opiate of the people, but to look for insight in the great religions of humanity.

My last stop was in Mexico City, where I climbed the Pyramid of the Moon and visited the shrine of Guadalupe and went to the Ballet Folklorico. I was already on a quest of understanding, a quest that I saw as very different from a quest of certainty. When you try to make sure, you become ever more unsure, I thought, but when you simply seek insight your quest is fruitful. I went on then to give a seminar on Faith and Doubt at Chicago in the Divinity School, where I connected faith with the quest of understanding and doubt with the quest of certainty. The circle of truths becomes smaller and smaller on the quest of certainty, I thought, but it becomes larger and more encompassing on the quest of understanding. I made ready then to go to Berkeley for the school year of 1969–1970 to work on my third book, on passing over to the great religions.

"How many centuries is it since a great religion shook the world?"[15] André Malraux asked, and that question became the starting point of my new project of passing over to the great religions, to Buddhism, to Christianity, to Islam. Each one of those three "shook the world," and if another religion of that magnitude has not come along in the meanwhile, still those three continue to shake the world. To pass over into them is to enter into that shaking of the foundations that they bring about. Buddhism shakes the foundations of self, bringing an enlightenment that carries us beyond the standpoint of self. Christianity shakes the foundations of life and death, bringing the revelation of a life that is eternal. Islam shakes the foundations of our will and purpose, bringing the revelation of a God whose will is accomplished in everything that happens.

I tried passing over into the lives of the founders, passing over to Gotama, to Jesus, to Mohammed. I saw each of them as going into solitude to gain insight and then coming back to the human circle to share the insight with others. I say "insight," meaning "enlightenment" for Gotama and "revelation" for Jesus and Mohammed. It is as though there is a common underlying experience of going into solitude and coming back again into the human circle but in each one a unique insight into that common experience. Solitude for Gotama is being alone that is being all one, an aloneness that becomes all oneness in the enlightenment of "no self" (*anatta*). Solitude for Jesus is being alone with the Alone whom he calls Abba, the Alone of "unconditional relation,"[16] as Martin Buber calls it, I and thou. Solitude for Mohammed is being alone with the Alone whom he calls Allah the Compassionate, the Merciful.

Coming back then into the human circle, Gotama spends the rest of his life teaching others to follow the way he has found. The remainder of his life was many years, until he finally died in his eighties. Jesus too, coming back into the human circle, spends his time teaching others to follow him in his relationship with God, but his time is short and he shows by his death and resurrection the way through death to eternal life. Mohammed has to flee from Mecca to Medina in order to continue sharing the revelation he has received. The return then to the human circle becomes the test of the teaching of each great religion, the test of a long and peaceful life, the test of death and resurrection, the test of flight (Hegira) or journey.

Lives are the key to the great religions, it seemed to me, for instance the life of Gandhi, who passed over from Hinduism to Christianity and Islam and came back again with new insight to Hinduism, "experimenting with truth,"[17] as he says. My own passing over to the great religions led to coming back with new insight to Christianity. I called my book, nevertheless, *The Way of All the Earth*, a phrase I found in the King James Version of the Bible corresponding to the phrase "the way of all flesh" in the Douay Version, meaning the way of common mortality.[18] I use it to mean the common experience of humanity and to imply that the great religions each consist of unique insight into the common experience of humanity. There is a depth in common experience, I want to say, that is revealed in the great religions.

Although *The Way of All the Earth* was well received in England and recently has been listed here as one of the best spiritual books of the century, I ran into some criticism at the time at the American Academy of Religion from those who wanted to approach the religions, especially Buddhism, in terms of spiritual disciplines, for instance Buddhist meditation. My own approach in terms of story, for instance the story of the Buddha, his withdrawal into solitude and his return to the human circle, led to the thought that his enlightenment came of an insight into the failure of the yogas, the failure of the spiritual disciplines. For those of Protestant background to whom spiritual disciplines and methods of meditation were a new discovery, it was very unwelcome to hear of the failure of such methods. All the same, I thought this insight into failure carries us into the very heart of Buddhism.

I began to enter a midlife crisis as I returned from Berkeley to Notre Dame and finished writing this book. My father had come to visit me in May of that year at Berkeley and I had taken him to my favorite haunts, there and in the Muir Woods and San Francisco and on to Yosemite and Reno. I think I was still at peace at that time, but I began to be restless, especially as I came back from the West. A married couple I had met in California came back with me as far as Denver. I remember our visit to the Grand Canyon, climbing down into the canyon and spending a sleepless night by a spring of water as people came up from below and down from above and all stopped for water. We learned the next day at Mesa Verde that the canyon, according to Indian legend, was the hole of the world where the dead went down and the newborn came up. My friends left me in Denver, and then I had a very lonely trip over the Great Plains that I afterwards called "the deadly clear path."

That was the crisis: I seemed to see the next twenty years laid out before me in deadly clarity. I found an alternate image at the time, nevertheless, that seemed an answer. Instead of the deadly clarity of seeing all the way to the horizon on the Great Plains, I thought of driving on the highway at night, seeing only a portion of the road in the car's headlights, and driving into that moving patch of light, going insight by insight into the future. I thought of Newman's prayer, "Lead Kindly Light,"

> Keep Thou my feet;
> I do not ask to see
> The distant scene—
> One step enough for me.[19]

Seeing twenty years ahead, imagining myself doing the same thing for the next twenty years, teaching at Notre Dame, was seeing "the distant scene." Instead I had to think of myself as going into the unknown, one step at a time, "one step enough for me."

It is true, I did spend the next twenty years, even the next thirty years, teaching at Notre Dame, but much else happened that I could not foresee at the time, and so the vision of driving on the highway at night, of going insight by insight into the future, has proved a true one. It is indeed the vision of a journey with God in time, being led by the "kindly light" of God, kindling my heart and illumining my mind. "Our heart is restless until it rest in thee," and there is rest in God in being led one step at a time. Still, I felt restless, for "I sometimes wish," as I had written in my diary, "that I had a human companion, visible and tangible," and it was that restlessness for human companionship that opened onto the unknown for me, though the unknown future actually held much else for me, especially voyages and travels.

> Two roads diverged in a wood, and I—
> I took the one less traveled by,[20]

Robert Frost's well-known lines were true for me, I took the road less traveled by, but I was haunted by "the road not taken." I had taken the road of a journey with God in time, but I was haunted by the road I had not taken, that of human intimacy in marriage and a family, the road more traveled by. The best answer I found was in Tolkien's trilogy, *a willingness to walk alone* that is open nevertheless to human companionship. A *will* to walk alone would exclude all human companionship, but a *willingness* to walk alone is open to human company. At each great turning point in Tolkien's story the main character, Frodo, has to be willing to walk alone, but as soon as he is willing he finds companionship after all, though he doesn't find marriage and family like Sam, his friend and servant.

In the end Frodo sails into the west with Bilbo and other friends and guides, and that seemed to me an image of eternal life, an image of the ending of my journey with God in time. I was invited to give the Thomas More Lectures at Yale in February 1971, and I found myself speaking out of this vision of a journey with the eternal in time. I was simply summing up my three books in the three lectures (later to be my fourth book, *Time and Myth*), but the journey with the eternal in time became the key to the answers to death I found in the first, the life stories in the second, and the great religions in the third. Usually, if you are living in your mind, the thing that brings you to living in your heart is love. For me, though, it was death that brought me into my heart, death and the hope of eternal life. All the same, living in my heart, though death led me there, left me open and vulnerable to love.

It was love that was on my mind as I went to the Kennedy Symposium in Washington, D.C., in October of 1971, the love of a woman I had met when I was in California, but the theme of the symposium was birth and death, and those invited were geneticists, behaviorists, and ethicists. I was there as an ethicist, and I met some remarkable others among the ethicists: I saw Jean Vanier again and I met Mother Teresa of Calcutta and I heard Elie Wiesel. Among the behaviorists I met B. F. Skinner and spoke with him about his forthcoming autobiography, asking him how he could write an autobiography if he did not have a self (he had rejected the concept of self in his *Science and Human Behavior*).[21] He looked at me with wonder and replied, "You write about the particulars of your life," and sure enough his autobiography appeared afterwards with the Shakespearean title, *Particulars of My Life*.[22] I didn't press him on the meaning of the word "my," but I find the concept of self guiding me in telling of the particulars of my life, "May I know me! May I know thee!"

My encounter with death was complete with the death of my father on Christmas Eve of 1971. I was there with him when he died in the hospital, and my brother and sister were there too. Only my brother was there with my mother when she died on July 31st of 1968, the day after I returned from South America. Your mother and father stand between you and death, and when they are gone you realize how they shielded you from death. You realize it most fully when they are both gone, as I did after the death of my father. During his last days my brother and sister and I took turns sitting up with him at night in the hospital. The exhaustion of that and of the funeral arrangements afterwards, together with the shock of his death and the sense of loss with both of them gone, my mother and my father, were perhaps enough to explain what happened afterwards—when I got back to Notre Dame I came down with pneumonia.

It was on January 1st of 1972 that I went into the infirmary with pneumonia. I had intended to fly that morning to LaCrosse for a wedding, that of my friends Bud Hammes and Barb Becker, but I was stopped at the door of the seminary where I was staying by Father Louis Putz and Monsignor John Egan and told I was going to the infirmary instead. There I was diagnosed with pneumonia, and I called my friends in LaCrosse from bed to tell them I could not come. The experience of pneumonia was a *V* experience, as I call it, going down one side of the *V* as life and hope were waning and then coming up the other side as life and hope were waxing again. I was reading *The Brothers Karamazov* those days in bed, and I was thinking about life and hope, "Where there is life, there is hope," and I thought the converse is also true, "Where there is hope, there is life." That seemed to be my experience of coming out of pneumonia, a rising hope and a rising energy of living that seemed to prepare me for a new life.

It was at this point that I found myself in the situation that Thomas Cole shows in the third of his paintings on *The Voyage of Life*. He names this one "Manhood," and he has the man kneeling in his storyboat and praying as he heads into the great rapids, and behind him in the darkened sky there is a figure of light. I imagine this was the point in life where Thomas Cole was himself when he did this painting. I was certainly heading into the great rapids myself, and I was praying to be guided and guarded, and I imagine there was a figure of light in the darkened sky behind me, listening to my prayer, or as I thought, voyaging with me, invisible at my side.

Thomas Cole, *The Voyage of Life: Manhood*, 1842. Courtesy of the National Gallery of Art, Washington, D.C. Copyright © 2003. Ailsa Mellon Bruce Fund 1971.16.3.

The Mystery of Encounter

Emerging from my encounter with death, I was vulnerable to an encounter with love. "The poem is lonely. It is lonely and *en route*. Its author stays with it," Paul Celan says. "Does this very fact not place the poem already here, at its inception, in the encounter, *in the mystery of encounter?*"[1] I was lonely and *en route*, I was on a journey in time and God was my only companion, and did this not place me, like the poem, in the encounter, in the mystery of encounter? My encounter with death had taught me about living in the heart, and now I had to learn what it is to love "with all your heart, and with all your soul, and with all your might."

For me then the mystery of encounter was twofold, the encounter with death and the encounter with love. I felt restless after my encounter with death. Learning to love God meant going from restlessness to rest, as in Saint Augustine's words, "Our heart is restless until it rest in thee." Meanwhile I was finding friends upon my way, as Tolkien says, when I least looked for it.[2] My restlessness was an uneasiness with my life as a journey in time with God as my only companion. The women friends I was finding upon my way I was seeing as possible companions on my journey. It was the restlessness I had already felt in 1968 at the prospect of my lone journey through South America, "I sometimes wish . . . that I had a human companion, visible and tangible." My answer now is that I didn't know then how real the journey can be in time and how real God's companionship can be. At the time, though, my answer was to find *rest in restlessness.*

As I saw it, the human spirit is essentially restless, and rest in restlessness is a Yes to the unquiet of the spirit. "The restlessness is like the unquiet of the sea, the constant motion of the waves," I wrote. "To be willingly restless is to be at rest; to be willingly unquiet is to be quiet. It is like a calm in which the sea becomes transparent to its depths."[3] Still, this was not yet the rest in God that Saint Augustine speaks of, "our heart is restless until it rest in thee," or that Dante speaks of, "his will is our peace." It was a willing acceptance of my own restlessness. "A willing restlessness is still restless, though, a willing unquiet still unquiet," I wrote. "The most one can say is that it is a rest in restlessness, a quiet in unquiet." I found something closer to rest and peace in reading Tolkien, much as I had found it earlier in reading the *Summa.*

It is true, what I found in reading Tolkien's trilogy was a sense of being on a journey in time and thus a rest in the restless movement of a journey. It was a reinforcement of my own vision of life as a journey in time with God as my companion on the way. So *rest in restlessness* thus understood, a journey with God in time, is my understanding even now of "until it rest in thee" and "his will is our peace." There is a stability for me in Tolkien's story, in the celibacy of Bilbo and Frodo, in the willingness of Frodo to walk alone. I saw the four spiritual truths I found in Tolkien in the mystery of encounter, "Things are meant; there are signs; the heart speaks; there is a way." I have lost count of the number of times I have read the trilogy, but every time I read it I find a sense of serenity and adventure, a serenity in the adventure.

I began writing *Time and Myth* in the summer of 1971, and I came upon a vision of things that carried me beyond the summing up I had done in the actual lectures in February. I was in New Haven again in the summer, and I heard Sister Margaret Farley say in conversation that she found a life in the Eucharist she believed could live through death. That sparked an insight for me. I saw that instead of asking "Is there a life after death?" we could ask "Is there a deeper life now that can live on through death?" That deeper life, I saw, would be the life of the spirit, the life of knowledge and love. So I introduced the idea in the first chapter and used it to interpret the epics. I made a distinction there between *the things of life* and *our relation to the things*, identifying the deeper life with the life of relation, of knowing and loving.

I broke off the writing of *Time and Myth* in the second chapter, writing about the ages of life. I had written the parts on childhood and youth, I believe, but the break came before I wrote the last section, "The Man and the Story of Death." What happened there was my father's death and my bout with pneumonia. I began the section with a quote from Dana's *Two Years before the Mast* about daybreak at sea giving one "a feeling of loneliness, of dread, and of melancholy foreboding,"[4] my own feeling when my mother and father had died and life had opened up before me all the way to death. Then I described five encounters with other persons, my meditation on the mystery of encounter: the encounter with a self-sacrificing person, with a self-absorbed person, with a person caught up in madness, with a person who truly sees and hears, and finally with a person who falls in love with me—I believe I was thinking in this last of the woman I met in California.

I came then in the third chapter to the struggle of flesh and spirit, the struggle I was experiencing at this time, and *The Brothers Karamazov*, the book I had been reading in those days in bed with pneumonia. I saw myself as a person of spirit, and the life of spirit as one of hope and peace and friends and intelligence, but the mystery of encounter had awakened in me the person of flesh and my task, as I saw it, was to integrate flesh and spirit, to become a whole person, to learn what it is to love "with all your heart, and with all your soul, and with all your might." How to do this? The only way I could see was to kiss the earth like Alyosha, to embrace mortal existence, but my heart was and is still in the life of the spirit, the life of hope and peace and friends and intelligence.

In the end, writing the conclusion and the preface, I came to the question "What kind of story are we in?" There is a sea-change in the things of our life, I concluded, due to our relationship with them, the life of our spirit. Our story then is that of a spiritual journey, a spiritual voyage. I loved reading and rereading Tolkien because of that sense of being on a journey, and I loved the thought of sailing into the west in the end like Bilbo and Frodo, a spiritual voyage into eternal life, "and again the sun went down in a burning red that faded into a grey mist; and into the mist a small ship passed away, twinkling with lights."[5] Living the life of the spirit, I believe, the life of hope and peace and friends and intelligence, I am living a life that is eternal, a life that will live on through death.

I was invited at this time to teach at Yale for a year (1972–1973) as a visiting professor (the Riggs Chair), and I was asked to design courses, two of them, Historic Responses to Death (now called Death and Rebirth) and Religion and Autobiography, courses I have since been teaching at Notre Dame. Of the other two, the Essence of Catholicism I taught only at Yale and Religion and Mysticism I taught once in a while afterwards at Notre Dame. That year at Yale was a year of decision for me, deciding whether to continue on the road I had taken in life or to take instead "the road not taken." I talked to Henri Nouwen, who was there at Yale that year, and I came to believe I didn't really want to take the road more traveled by, the road of marriage and family. My heart, I came to believe, was really in the road I had taken, the road less traveled by, my journey in time with God as my companion on the way. I was with Henri and my friend Robert Jay Lifton and others in a discussion group at Yale, and I presented to them my ideas about living a spiritual life that could live on through death, an inner life that is eternal.

My decision was confirmed when I went to the Holy Land in the summer of 1974 for the Hope Seminar of Jews and Christians and Muslims. I had originally intended to go to this seminar just to give some talks, as I had been asked, and to spend the rest of the time writing. But even before I went I changed my mind and decided to make this a time of pilgrimage. And that is what it turned out to be. "When you enter upon a journey like this," I wrote in my diary, "the journey takes you." I was with my sister and with Rita Jansen, a former student of mine, and others I knew in that way. One of the Jews in our group, Hayim, befriended me and spoke to me of "your studies," giving me a sense of study as a spiritual quest. One of the Muslims, Abd-el-Jalil, took me to a little Sufi mosque in the Old City of Jerusalem, where the Sufis danced, chanting "Allah . . . Allah" as if forgetting all but God—I thought of "the cloud of forgetting"[6] in *The Cloud of Unknowing*. But the really transforming experience for me came when we camped by the Sea of Galilee and I went a little apart and sat reading the Beatitudes in the Gospel of Matthew. It was as if I were meeting Christ and he were saying "Follow me!"[7] I realized I am a Christian and not simply a universal man who can understand all the religions.

In the Sinai desert we traveled to the oasis of El Firan and took the old pilgrim's walk to Mount Sinai and Saint Catherine's monastery. We met a Bedouin girl, about thirteen years old, herding goats, who played the flute for us but from a distance and without lifting her veil. After a while she turned aside, waving goodbye, playing her flute, the goats following.[8] Her distance from us was like that of our Bedouin guide. When we invited him to come with us back to Jerusalem, he refused saying, "I'm happy here. But if I saw Jerusalem I wouldn't be happy any more."[9] When I returned to the Holy Land in the summer of 1976, this time again with people I knew, such as Claire Wing, a former student of mine, I had another encounter with the Bedouin in the Sinai. I was sitting under a palm tree at Dahab on the Gulf of Eilat (the Gulf of Akaba), writing in my diary, when a woman approached me and asked, "How many children do you have?" I heard myself saying to her, "Many."[10] Afterwards, as I thought of it, my answer seemed to me somehow inspired: physically I had no children and yet spiritually I had many children, teaching for all these years.

I met a blind man when I was in Jerusalem this second time, a young blind man with a seeing-eye dog. I helped him cross the street at a somewhat complex crossroads, and then he asked me where I was going. "To Hebrew University," I said, "but I don't know how to get there from here." Then he said "Come with me!" and with the dog leading, him following and then me, we walked to Hebrew University. I knew I was in a parable, for "if the blind lead the blind, both shall fall into the ditch,"[11] but what if the seeing lead the blind, as I led him at the crossroads, and what if the blind lead the seeing, as he led me? I wrote a song about this later,

> If the blind
> lead the blind,
> all fall down
> into the pit,
> but if the seeing
> lead the blind,
> then give us light
> and we will walk
> into the dark,
> and if the blind
> lead the seeing,
> we will walk
> and will find light
> instead of dark.[12]

I went from Jerusalem to Oxford, where I was invited to give the Sarum Lectures in the fall of 1976, "The Reasons of the Heart." I began with the story of Lawrence of Arabia encountering an old Bedouin in the desert, who said to him, "The love is from God and of God and towards God."[13] For a long time, as I was writing these lectures beforehand, I had nothing but this story and this saying, and I simply sat, contemplating its meaning. Then at last the writing began to move forward. When I gave the lectures at Oxford, I didn't read them, to the surprise of some, but simply spoke from an outline. I did begin with this story, though, and this saying. I connected the love with the deep loneliness of the human condition, citing the African love song, "I walk alone."[14] As I saw it, the loneliness becomes the love, or the yearning in the loneliness becomes the love, and the spiritual journey begins with the loneliness, like Dante in the beginning of *The Divine Comedy,* "lost in a dark wood," and ends in the love, like Dante at the end, caught up in "the love that moves the sun and the other stars."[15]

So "Faith is God sensible to the heart," as Pascal says, "sensible," that is perceptible, as we go from loneliness to love, and "the heart has reasons that reason does not know,"[16] reasons hidden in our loneliness, but these reasons of the heart, I wanted to say, can become known to the mind, known as we go from loneliness to love. As God becomes sensible to the heart, we go from the common notion of God, according to which everything that happens is the will of God, to the notion of God found in the Gospels, that all things are possible to God, and in the Gospel of John, that God is spirit. I understood this last to mean that God acts spiritually, by kindling the heart and illumining the mind. As God becomes sensible to the heart, we come to realize that being "alone with the Alone" really means being unalone, and our intimacy with God is like no other intimacy, so that only God can enter into our soul. We come to realize then that God is our heart's desire, God is what our heart desires, I mean, and that explains much that happens in human relations, what we are seeking and finding in one another.

"There is no one here who has an understanding for me in full," I quoted from Kafka's diary. "To have even one who had this understanding, for instance a woman, would be to have support from every side. It would be to have God."[17] That was a perfect description of my own feeling of heart's desire. I thought I had found a woman like this, who had this understanding, and then I lost her again. Or she was like mystery that "shows itself and at the same time withdraws."[18] So I spoke in the lectures of "soul," the side of us that connects with mystery, and I meditated on the Gospel sayings, "He who finds his soul will lose it" and "He who loses his soul for my sake will find it."[19] What I came to believe, though, or to understand, was that only God can have this understanding for us "in full," *im ganzen* as Kafka says, and that the heart's yearning is ultimately for God, and that we have to release one another from the demand for full understanding.

I can only look to God, I realized, to find "an understanding for me in full." When I first arrived in the Holy Land in 1974, I had seen a man holding his little daughter, about two years old, while she was pinching his cheek and saying "Abba, Abba, Abba." And when I was there again in 1976, I had seen a little boy, all alone, calling out "Abba . . . Abba."[20] These two images, one of intimacy and one of distance, came together in my mind as I thought of our relation with God. What happens in Christianity, I believe, is that we enter into the "unconditional relation,"[21] as Martin Buber calls it, of Jesus with his God, whom he calls Abba. "I in them and thou in me"[22] is the formula in the Gospel of John, Jesus in the disciples and Abba in Jesus. So our relation with God, I concluded in the last lecture, is both indwelling and "I and thou."

My sense of being on a journey with God in time became more vivid in my second journey through South America in 1978, ending with a voyage up the Amazon. This time, instead of going down the east side of South America and coming up the west side, I went down the west side and came up the east side, giving talks again to the Holy Cross people in Chile, the priests and brothers and lay volunteers. I got an ear infection, staying overnight at a Holy Cross school in Santiago, sleeping in damp bedding. The ear infection stayed with me as I went on to Rio and to Brasilia and on to Belem at the mouth of the Amazon. I managed, after waiting a couple of days at Belem, to get passage with Mary Beckman, a former student of mine, on a riverboat named *Lobo d'Almada,* actually a seagoing vessel, to travel the thousand-mile voyage up the Amazon to Manaus, where the Rio Negro flows into the Amazon.

As our riverboat entered the Amazon, many poor people in small boats rowed out to us, and people on the riverboat threw clothes to them in the water. As I watched this happening, the person next to me said, "Do you see who is throwing the clothes?" I looked and saw that it was the poor people who slept in hammocks on the riverboat, while the richer people who slept in cabins like myself were only watching. I was thinking of Karl Marx, his very brief Theses on Feuerbach, where he says the human essence is not in the individual but in the ensemble of the social relations. I thought also of Freud, how he might say the human essence is not in the individual but in man and woman together. My own thought, nevertheless, was that the human essence is in the individual, and I found myself spending time with the people from the hammocks as well as the people from the cabins, as if we were all one.

Our voyage lasted five days, and I kept a very careful log, using a map of the Amazon. That map became a conversation piece on the riverboat. People would stop and ask to look at the map and then would engage in conversation. I still have the map and find I have marked on it the dates and times of our stops along the river. I later looked up our ship in *Lloyd's Register of Shipping* and found it was listed as a "twin-screw motorship" with accommodation for 398 passengers. We started at Belem on Wednesday, July 26, 1978, at 10:00 A.M., and then according to my map we came to Almeirim at 5:15 P.M. on Thursday, to Monte Alegre at 7:45 A.M. and to Santarem at 2:35 P.M. (time moved back an hour) on Friday, to Obidos at 3:00 A.M. and to Parintins at 1:30 P.M. on Saturday, and we arrived at Manaus on Sunday at 5:00 P.M.[23] At one point along the way we saw a hut on the river with a sign above the door saying "Faith in God" (*Fe em Deus*).

My ear infection was still with me, and the last night on the boat when people were dancing the Samba and urging me to join in the dance, I was so sick I went down to my cabin and lay on my bunk sweating. The next day, when we arrived at Manaus, the fever had left me.

I persuaded a group of Brasilian medical students who were with me on the riverboat to help me find a little chapel called the Church of the Poor Devil (*Igreja do Pobre Diabo*). I had come across mention of it in a guidebook and I was intrigued by the name. We found it in a neighborhood of Manaus near a military hospital. It was very small, a little wedding chapel as I learned, and its official name was Chapel of Santo Antonio, the saint who was patron of weddings in Brazil. I wondered, though, how it got its popular name, the Church of the Poor Devil. Who was the Poor Devil? I could find no answers then, but later I became so enamored of the name and intrigued by it that I decided to name a book for it, *The Church of the Poor Devil*, a book about the religion of the poor. When I decided on that name, I realized I had to return and find out who the Poor Devil was.

I did return two years later, in 1980, this time flying direct to Manaus from Los Angeles (I was on sabbatical in Berkeley). A friend from Berkeley came with me, Elizabeth Carr, and we came in June to be at the festival of Santo Antonio when the chapel would be open. I came with a question, "Who was the Poor Devil?" and with a vision of things based on a passage I found in Tolkien about "rekindling hearts in a world that grows chill." It is a passage where the wizard Gandalf receives a ring on coming to Middle Earth:

> "Take this ring, Master," he said, "for your labours will be heavy; but it will support you in the weariness that you have taken upon yourself. For this is the Ring of Fire, and with it you may rekindle hearts in a world that grows chill."[24]

I had come to this vision, and with it the idea of the book, after refusing an offer to come and teach at Stonybrook in New York in January 1978, before I had ever discovered the chapel of the Poor Devil. The decision led to a release of creative energy. I didn't realize how much energy was bound up in making the decision. When it was released, I sat down and outlined six chapters for the book that later became *The Church of the Poor Devil.*

That passage about rekindling hearts had spoken to my heart earlier when I presided at a wedding and on the way back was thinking of my own vocation in life. My calling was indeed to "rekindle hearts in a world that grows chill." Now as I studied the Church of the Poor Devil, I was thinking of a world growing chill and of rekindling hearts. I saw the little chapel as an embodiment of *religion popular* as my friend and former student Diego Irarrazaval calls it, "the sigh of the oppressed," as Marx says, "the heart of a heartless world, and the soul of soulless conditions."[25] I saw what I was doing myself as *passing over* to the religion of the poor and *coming back* with new insight to my own standpoint of personal religion.

But who was the Poor Devil? I found a metal plaque had been set on the door of the chapel reading, "Chapel of Santo Antonio, built for Cordolina Rosa de Viterbo, given to the diocese on November 28, 1897, 'Church of the Poor Devil,' Cultural Foundation of the Amazon." Then I learned from local scholars Geraldo Pinheiro and Mario Ypiranga that Cordolina lived with a man called Antonio Jose da Costa, who owned a cabaret and called himself "the Poor Devil" *(o Pobre Diabo)* and that after his death and their deathbed marriage Cordolina called herself "the Poor Devil" *(a Pobre Diaba).* And I learned she had a son also named Antonio. I began to see in this the outlines of a play, especially when another female character was introduced. Geraldo Pinheiro asked me if I would like to meet the black woman who presided over the African rites. I heard myself saying I would be fascinated—I had no idea there were African rites. Her name was Zulmira, and her counterpart in Cordolina's time was named Joana. Now I had all the characters for a play, or as it turned out a musical, Cordolina, Antonio, Joana, and Santo Antonio.

My visit to Zulmira was at night with Geraldo Pinheiro and Sister Evelina Trindade, who was my interpreter. I thought of Saul going to visit the witch of Endor. Zulmira was at first reluctant to see us, but when she learned I was a *padre*, she welcomed us, saying that no *padre* had been there since the nineteenth century. I was worried at that, asking myself what I was doing. She showed us the *barracao* where the African rites were held. There I saw a model of the chapel of the Poor Devil surrounded by statues of saints, whom Zulmira explained were also African gods and goddesses. Each figure had two names, that of a Catholic saint and that of an African god or goddess. I saw also a picture and shrine of Jemanja, the great goddess, who corresponded, according to Zulmira, to the Virgin Mary. She was the goddess of the Amazon and also of the sea, and offerings were left for her on the shore at Rio, I learned, that the tide would take out to sea.

So the mystery of encounter involved me in an encounter with popular religion as well as with the great religions, and an encounter with women as well as with men, but my *thou* was never really other than God, and my journey was always a journey with God in time. "So, waiting, I have won from you the end: God's presence in each element,"[26] Goethe's saying is the epigraph of Martin Buber's *I and Thou*. According to Buber the *thou* of a life can be the *thou* of dialogue, as it was for Socrates, or the *thou* of nature, as it was for Goethe, or the eternal *thou*, as it was for Jesus, or, we could add, the *thou* of love, as it was for Dante. I found the *thou* of dialogue at Notre Dame and at Yale and at Oxford, and I found the *thou* of nature on the Amazon, and I found the *thou* of love in friendships, but I think the *thou* of my life is the eternal *thou*. I was indeed like the man in Thomas Cole's painting, kneeling in my storyboat as it went into the rapids, praying to a figure of light in the sky above and behind. The great rapids for me were the roads not taken in life, the possibilities of human companionship on my journey. I had to be willing to walk alone with God, but as soon as ever I was willing to walk alone I always found human company after all. Still, my journey was ever a journey in time and God was always my companion on the way.

The Mystery of Our Loneliness

"Now I see the mystery of your loneliness."
—Shakespeare in
All's Well That Ends Well

"Now I see the mystery of your loneliness,"[1] the Countess says to Helena in *All's Well That Ends Well*, meaning now I see the secret of your loneliness, that you are in love with my son Bertram. Now I see the mystery of our loneliness, I could say too, meaning now I see the secret of our loneliness, that we are in love with God. Saying this is like Saint Augustine in his *Confessions* saying "our heart is restless until it rest in thee."

Our loneliness, as I understand it, is a combination of being alone and yearning to be unalone. We feel it especially in the boundary situations of life such as facing the prospect of death. The love of God, I think, is there in that yearning. It is as though we love with a love we do not know, not knowing the yearning is for God. Now I see the mystery of our loneliness, I want to say, seeing the mystery of my own loneliness. I see it now as I write this autobiography, and I saw it at this point in my life, after my encounter with death and my encounter with love. I saw it as I wrote about the reasons of the heart, but at this later point in my life, the 1980s and my fifties, I saw it as *wisdom*. My conception of wisdom is to know the secret of our loneliness, to know the human heart is in love with God. It starts as knowing my own heart, knowing I am in love with God.

Love of God, I gather from Spinoza, is simply joy at the thought of God, for me joy at the thought of being on a journey with God in time. There are growing pains, nevertheless, ih learning to love "with all your heart, and with all your soul, and with all your might." Reading Spinoza is like reading the *Summa:* there is a peace of mind in his vision of God as the reality underlying everything. That peace is the joy of loving God with all your mind. To learn to love with all your heart and soul, though, is a long journey, I have found. You have to become vulnerable to love and death. Wisdom then is a knowing that comes of loving, a loving that comes of being vulnerable as God is vulnerable. The journey with God in time then is a companionship with God in love and death.

I went again on a journey to find wisdom, this time to the historic shrine of Holy Wisdom, the Ayasofya in Istanbul. It was a church for a thousand years, the Hagia Sophia, a mosque for five hundred years, the Ayasofya, and now an empty monument. I took the name Ayasofya, the Turkish derivative from the Greek Hagia Sophia, and began to use it as personal name for the figure of Wisdom in the Bible. I called her Ayasofya and entered into an *I and thou* with her, even dedicating to her the book I afterwards wrote on the experience, and later writing a songcycle to her.

Is Holy Wisdom a person, I asked myself, or only a personification of divine wisdom? I found a prayer to her in the Liturgy of the Hours,

> Wisdom of God,
> be with me,
> always at work in me.[2]

And I found three different views among the saints, that of Saint Athanasius that Christ is the Wisdom of God, that of Saint Irenaeus that Wisdom is the Holy Spirit, and that of Saint Augustine that Wisdom is the divine essence.[3] I am able to pray to Holy Wisdom without resolving the question in my mind, and indeed generally to pray without asking myself, Am I praying to the Father or to the Son or to the Holy Spirit? That is so, though I believe the Lord's Prayer is addressed to the Father, the God of Jesus, whom he called Abba, and not as Saint Thomas says to all three persons of the Trinity.[4] Anyway, I am able to pray to God without asking who it is, and I am able to pray to Holy Wisdom without asking who she is. My prayer is my *I and thou* with her.

There was an encompassing peace, I found, in the Ayasofya, and I used to visit every day of the ten days I spent in Istanbul, so much so that Aksen, who offered me hospitality there, remarked "You are in love with Ayasofya." I had known Aksen's sister Aysen in America, as she was married to Greg Wolff and I knew the Wolff family, and Aysen had written to her sisters Aksen and Gulsen of my coming. So I stayed only one night in a little hotel in Istanbul before they took me in, the Paksoy family, and I stayed in Gulsen's apartment while she stayed with the family. The word *sen* (pronounced "shen") in Turkish means "smile." I called the three sisters in my own mind "the three *sens*," Aksen "white smile," Aysen "smiling moon," and Gulsen "smiling rose," and their hospitality was as warm and beautiful as their names.

"Turn to life! God is in your heart!" Aksen said to me when she learned of celibacy. She was not yet married herself and she thought I should contemplate marriage, also become a Muslim, and stay in Istanbul. She took me on a tour of the mosques in Istanbul and introduced me to a professor at Istanbul University who engaged me in conversations about Christianity and Islam. He was constantly fingering his prayer beads, and when I was leaving he gave them to me. I stole a glance at his fingers, after he had given me the beads, but his fingers were still, not nervously twitching as if the beads had been worry beads. So I was all the more impressed with his devotion. All the same, what Aksen said was true of me, "You are in love with Ayasofya."

I named the book I wrote about this experience *The House of Wisdom*, thinking of the passage in Proverbs that is echoed in Lawrence of Arabia's *Seven Pillars of Wisdom*, "Wisdom has built her house, she has set up her seven pillars."[5] The Ayasofya in Istanbul has a peace about it you can feel, the peace of over a thousand years of prayer. After I first visited there, I was in the nearby Blue Mosque, and I met a young Dutchman who pointed to the Ayasofya in the distance and asked "Have you been there?" "It's hard to leave, isn't it?" he said. To me too it seemed the Ayasofya retained its power, the peace of all those years of prayer, though it was no longer a church or a mosque. I associated the figure of Wisdom with that peace.

I suppose it was my experience with the Church of the Poor Devil that made me expect so much significance from a place. So the epi-

graph of each chapter of this book on Wisdom has to do with signifi-
cant place, "on returning to my hill of dreams," "on coming into Ayasofya in Istanbul," "on starting on a wanderyear of soul," "on going
from station to station in the Rothko Chapel," "on arriving at a point
of inflection," "on sitting in the Meditation Room at the UN," "on
walking in the woods at World's End." My hill of dreams is where I
found my spiritual adventure; the Ayasofya is where I found the encompassing peace of Holy Wisdom; a wanderyear of soul is an image
of my journey with God in time; the stations of the cross in the
Rothko Chapel are my entry into the final journey of Christ; the point
of inflection is the turning point of my own journey; the Meditation
Room at the UN is a place of peace for me like the Ayasofya and the
Rothko Chapel; and the woods at World's End are an image of my
journey's end.

But what is wisdom? It is a knowing that comes of loving, I gathered. There is a distinction between knowing and loving: knowing is
taking things in, I had learned from Saint Thomas,[6] and loving is
going out to things. The distinction can become a separation between
the speculative realm of knowing and the practical realm of loving, as
in Kant's exclamation, "the starry heavens above me and the moral law
within me!"[7] That distinction was at first a separation also for Saint
Thomas, I found, but later became a unity in distinction, *distinguer
pour unir*, "distinguish to unite."[8] A knowing that comes of loving,
therefore, and a loving that leads to knowing. Life is about learning to
love, I began to see, and about the learning that comes of loving.

Knowing and loving are spirit; seeing and feeling are sense. Seeing
corresponds to knowing, and feeling to loving, and so the sense image
of spirit here is eyes and heart. "My eyes and my heart will be there for
all time,"[9] words of God to Solomon in a dream, are the epigraph then
of my book on wisdom. Ayasofya, the figure of Holy Wisdom, I take

to be the eyes and heart of God. Those words to Solomon in his dream are a promise to be there in the temple he built, to be there to answer prayer. My experience in the Ayasofya in Istanbul, the encompassing peace I found, was an experience of eyes and heart, my eyes seeing the encompassing space and my heart feeling the pervading peace. It was an experience of sense with an overlay of spirit, seeing with an overlay of knowing, feeling with an overlay of loving. My eyes and my heart were there as they were also in the Rothko and in the Meditation Room.

There is nothing wiser than a circle, it is said. "You have noticed that everything an Indian does is in a circle," Black Elk says, "and that is because the Power of the World always works in circles, and everything tries to be round."[10] So it is with wisdom. There is a great circle of love coming from God and going to God, and wisdom is knowing "The love is from God and of God and towards God," as the old Bedouin said to Lawrence of Arabia. It is knowing we are all in love with God, I have come to believe, and the love comes from God and returns to God. It is seeing that comes of feeling, knowing that comes of loving. It is seeing with God's eyes, I believe, and feeling with God's heart.

One night in Istanbul I tried to walk all the way from the Paksoy family apartment to Gulsen's apartment where I was staying. The two sisters, Aksen and Gulsen, gave me careful directions but I became lost, walking by mistake on the bridge over the Bosphorus, the bridge that goes from Europe to Asia. Eventually I retraced my steps and started over, this time following the directions more carefully. All the time I was praying, wandering alone at night in Istanbul. The experience became an image for me of my journey with God in time. I was learning to love "with all your heart" as well as "with all your mind," but I had still to learn to love "with all your soul, and with all your might." Meanwhile I found myself praying to Holy Wisdom not to desert me, not to give me over to foolishness, to unseeing and unfeeling, to unloving.

It was three years later, in 1985, when I went on my third pilgrimage to Jerusalem, that I began to learn what it is to love "with all your soul." Sister Marie Goldstein invited me again to the Hope Seminar of Jews and Christians and Muslims, as she had before, but this time the seminar was not so much a meeting of the three religions as it was a Christian pilgrimage to the Holy Land. All the same, I had a very real encounter with Judaism in some young friends who were there in Jerusalem trying to recover their Jewish roots, and with Islam in a journey afterwards from Jerusalem to Cairo. Learning to love "with all your soul," if we make a distinction between self and soul, is learning to go beyond the standpoint of self.

Passing over, I suppose, is always going beyond the standpoint of self to that of another, and coming back is always returning to the standpoint of self. To love "with all your soul," though, is actually to live in a standpoint more comprehensive than that of self. It is to go from will to willingness, from hope to hopefulness. I had already come to the distinction between self and soul (in *A Search for God in Time and Memory*) and between will and willingness (in *The Reasons of the Heart*). What I came to now was that between hope and hopefulness, or in Jean Giono's terms, between *espoir* and *esperance*.[11] I read his little book *The Man Who Planted Trees*, or "The Man Who Planted Hope and Grew Happiness."[12] Hope (*espoir*) is setting your heart on someone or something; hopefulness (*esperance*) is being open to the mystery, being open, let me say now, to the mystery of our loneliness.

Hope (*espoir*) then is setting my heart on someone or something that I think will take away my loneliness; hopefulness (*esperance*) is opening my heart to the mystery of our loneliness, to the love of God, knowing we are in love with God and only the joy of being on a journey with God can make us unalone. There is a sadness in our loneliness, in simply being alone and wanting to be unalone, and a gladness in the love of God, in being "alone with the Alone."[13] For me Spinoza was a great help here, his idea that love of God is simply joy at the thought of God, and also Meister Eckhart, his idea of "wandering joy,"[14] which I take to be joy at the thought of being on a journey with God in time.

My journeys to Jerusalem, then, were the subject of my next book, *The Homing Spirit*. I took the first one (in 1974) to be a pilgrimage of the mind, the second (in 1976) to be a pilgrimage of the heart, and the third (in 1985) to be a pilgrimage of the soul. I was seeing them as a process of learning to love "with all your mind" and "with all your heart" and "with all your soul." This was retrospect, but it seems to be true to the experience, for instance of the second, which took place at the time I was writing *The Reasons of the Heart*. Passing over into Judaism and Islam, as I was doing on these journeys, and coming back with new insight into Christianity, I always came back to myself, but self became ever richer in the process, until it became indeed self endowed with soul. I think of a passage in Tolkien, "If your hurts grieve you still and the memory of your burden is heavy, then you may pass into the West, until all your wounds and weariness are healed."[15]

There are hurts and burden and wounds and weariness in the standpoint of self, I know, and there is healing and "passing into the West" in the standpoint of self endowed with soul. Peace was the object of each pilgrimage to Jerusalem, as I saw it, peace of mind, peace of heart, and ultimately peace of soul. I did find a peace of mind in that first pilgrimage in the simplicity of following Christ. I have come to realize that Christianity is not a story but a relationship, the relationship of Jesus with his God, Abba, and us entering and living in that relationship. There is a story, of course, a story of birth and death and resurrection, but the essence of Christianity is not in the story but in the relationship. So I came to understand following Christ as entering into his relationship with God. "I am ascending to my Father and your Father," he says to Mary Magdalene, "to my God and your God."[16]

I found a peace of heart then in the second pilgrimage, when I was exploring the reasons of the heart, meditating on the paradox of Christianity, that one who finds his heart's desire will lose it and one who loses it "for my sake" will find it. The finding and losing, I came to see, is not of the true heart's desire. It is rather of the desire Shaw is speaking of when he says "There are two tragedies in life. One is not to get your heart's desire. The other is to get it."[17] Setting my heart on someone or something, I come to loss, I do not get it and am disappointed, or else, as he says, I get it and am disappointed. What I can learn from disappointment, I realized, is "God is my desire,"[18] as Tolstoy wrote in his diary, my heart's desire is for God. That is how one who loses it "for my sake" will find it. I come then to that simple joy at the thought of being on a journey with God in time.

Or it would be truer to say I was thinking about these things at the time. I did indeed find a peace of mind in a settled vision and a peace of heart in following my heart's desire, but peace of soul eluded me on my third pilgrimage, for it required a "letting be" and an "openness to the mystery," and I was like Crazy Horse as Larry McMurtry describes him, "yearning for a woman he couldn't have."[19] I spoke of peace of soul in *The Homing Spirit* and I knew it required a detachment, the thing Meister Eckhart is always talking about. I knew the parable of Saint John of the Cross about the bird held by a thread,[20] how the bird cannot fly until the thread is broken. Yet it was only some years later that the thread was finally broken for me and I came at last to peace of soul.

Meanwhile I traveled from Jerusalem to Cairo, and I went from there to the desert monastery of Saint Macarius halfway up to Alexandria. It was a Coptic monastery, very friendly and ecumenical, and I learned there to my surprise, "The single requirement the spiritual father lays down for the acceptance of a postulant is that he should have sensed within his heart, even though it be only once, a feeling of love for God."[21] Does this mean, I asked myself, that only a happy few have this feeling? Everyone has such a feeling, I thought, rather, for everyone's heart is restless until it rests in God, but not everyone is conscious of it nor does everyone name it love of God. I began to see then how the spiritual journey is a coming to awareness of the love that comes from God and goes to God, getting caught up in the great circle of love—we are caught up in it, but the journey is a process of becoming aware of it.

I was seeking peace of soul then from this point on. "Seek peace and ensue it"[22] I took as my motto. I went on my third journey to Santiago in Chile at this time: the first was in 1968, the second in 1978, and the third in 1988, each time to give a series of talks to the Holy Cross Fathers and their associates working in Chile. I was speaking to them of peace, the outer peace of "an unviolent way of life" as I called it, and the inner peace of mind and heart that I had found and the peace of soul that I was still seeking. Each time I went to Chile I also went to Peru and visited Macchu Picchu, the ruins of an Inca city of refuge in the Andes. Seeing the sunrise there and the sunset, the first time I came there, I saw a vision of the peace I was seeking. At sunset the llamas came in and formed a kind of circle in the plaza of the ruined city, where they settled in for the night, and then at sunrise they rose again and went out to graze for the day.

It was magical that first time, almost as if the Incas were to return, but the second time it was a mirror of the human essence, the thing I was thinking about on that second journey which included my voyage up the Amazon. It was that second time in the spirit of Pablo Neruda's poem *The Heights of Macchu Picchu.* My thoughts were on the human essence, is it in the ensemble of the social relations as Marx says, or is it in man and woman together as perhaps Freud would say, or is it in the individual as Kierkegaard would say? My own feeling, both at Macchu Picchu and later on the Amazon, in spite of these reflections on the ensemble of the social relations and on the wholeness of man and woman together, was that the human essence is in the individual.

My third journey to Macchu Picchu then was "a vehicle of Mystery," as Tolkien says, "The Magical, the fairy-story, may be used as a *Mirour de l'Omme;* and it may (but not so easily) be made a vehicle of Mystery."[23] I was actually thinking of these categories of Tolkien's at the time, the magical, the mirror, and the mystery. As I see it now, the mystery of our lives is twofold: the mystery of encounter and the mystery of our loneliness. All I was doing on this third journey was staying in a little hotel in Cuzco and contemplating the mystery of encounter and the mystery of our loneliness and going from there on a little train in the mountains to Macchu Picchu. My contemplation carried me to the edge of a peace of soul, but I still lacked the detachment to go over the edge.

My book written at this time, *The Peace of the Present,* was about "an unviolent way of life," and the title came from Shakespeare's *Tempest* where to "work the peace of the present"[24] is to calm the storm. I began speaking of "heart's desire" as I call it, connecting it with inner peace, as in Dante's saying, "his will is our peace," and contrasting it with "mimetic desire" that René Girard connects with violence. I had a conversation once with Girard—we had been on a panel together.

He said all desire is mimetic: we see what others want and we want what they want, and "heart's desire" is not really desire but inner peace. I wanted to say nevertheless it is desire, the deepest yearning of the heart, though inner peace is the sign, the criterion, of being on the road of the heart's desire.

It is "the peace of the presence" that calms the storm, according to another reading of *The Tempest.* I thought of my friend David Daube and his reading of the "I am" sayings of the Gospel as expressions of the Shekinah, the divine presence. According to David, when Jesus says "I am" without anything following, such as "the way, the truth, and the life," he is saying "God is here," not indeed pointing to himself but to the presence itself. The translations have him saying "It is I" or "I am he," but the original has simply "I am." There is a moment in the Gospel of Mark when he actually calms the storm and another moment when he walks on the water and says, "Take heart, it is I, have no fear" or rather, "Take heart, I am; have no fear."[25] So he calms the storm, and he calms fear itself with the peace of the presence.

Violence is mimetic, I agreed with Girard, we do unto others as has been done unto us—thus stroke and counterstroke in Northern Ireland, in the Holy Land, in Bosnia, thus too the abused in a family become in turn abusers unless the cycle of violence is broken, unless we learn to do unto others as we would have them do unto us. My friend Erik Erikson, speaking at our meeting on Cape Cod in 1980 of the Galilean sayings of Jesus, pointed out how the Golden Rule, as Jesus formulated it, leads us into our own inwardness to ask what we would have others do unto us, to ask, I would say, about the heart's desire. Mimetic desire and heart's desire are related, I gathered, as violent and unviolent ways of life.

I concluded then in my inaugural lecture "The Sense of I in Christianity," included as a chapter in *The Peace of the Present,* to a vision of participation rather than of substitutionary atonement. There are two interpretations of Christianity, I thought, one in which Christ takes our place, that of substitutionary atonement, and the other in which we take his place, that of participation, "it is no longer I who live, but Christ who lives in me."[26] Girard has it that substitutionary atonement is a return to the mythology of the scapegoat. I hesitate to reject substitutionary atonement so strongly myself, though my understanding of atonement is an at-one-ment of us entering into Christ's relation with God, "my God and your God," "my Father and your Father." I thought (I said this in class rather than in writing) we could say the two interpretations were like waves and particles in physics, two images of the same reality.

So the mystery of our loneliness is the mystery of our love and longing for God, and it is fulfilled in us entering into the relationship of Jesus with the God he calls Abba, "my God and your God," as he says to Mary Magdalen, "my Father and your Father." If the love of God is simply joy at the thought of God, as I have learned from Spinoza, this means an underlying joy in a life. That is what I have found in spite of the fear and weariness and sadness of a life, an underlying joy, a joy at the thought of God with me on my journey in time. "Under all there was a great joy," as Tolkien says: "a fountain of mirth enough to set a kingdom laughing, were it to gush forth."[27]

The Road That Goes Ever On

> *"Perhaps my best years are gone, but I wouldn't want them back,*
> *not with the fire in me now."*
>
> —Samuel Beckett

The Road Goes Ever On is the title of a song cycle by Tolkien with music by Donald Swann. It has been an inspiration to me to write song cycles in these later years, and all my later books have song cycles or song and dance cycles at the end. Writing the music for these cycles and performing them with singers and dancers and myself on the piano has been my return to the way of music, my return to my "road not taken," as my road taken has been the way of words. All this has happened for me in the 1990s and has carried on into the 2000s, my sixties and into my seventies.

"He used often to say there was only one Road," Frodo says, quoting Bilbo; "that it was like a great river: its springs were at every doorstep, and every path was its tributary."[1] That is the road that goes ever on. My tributary path is the way of words, and I enter the great river as my path joins the way of music. This road then goes on and on, but my earthly life comes to an end. "Our span is seventy years or eighty for those who are strong."[2] It is eternal life that goes ever on, and I have learned from the Gospel of John that eternal life begins already now. So it is true to speak of eternal life as a road that goes ever on. Eternal life, though, is the life of the love of God, to love "with all your heart, and with all your soul, and with all your might." I learned earlier in my life to love with all my mind, and then later with all my heart, but in these last years I have learned to love with all my soul and with all my might. It takes a detachment in love, I believe, to love "with all your soul," a detachment I have been very late in learning, but there is a connection with music in loving "with all your might," as when it is said "David danced before the Lord with all his might."[3]

It is the element of detachment in love that I have had the hardest time learning in these late years. "A detached man, Eckhart says, experiences such a joy that no one would be able to tear it away from him," I read in Reiner Schürmann's book on Meister Eckhart. "But such a man remains unsettled. He who has let himself be, and who has let God be, lives in wandering joy, or joy without a cause."[4] I thought to find "wandering joy" in the sense of being on a journey with God in time, and I did find joy there. Yet the detachment eluded me, as long as I was like Crazy Horse "yearning for a woman he couldn't have." It was only after she broke off our long friendship (in 1996) that I began slowly to learn detachment. I often prayed the prayer I found in *Dakota,* "Keep me friendly to myself, keep me gentle in disappointment,"[5] and my prayer was answered.

To love "with all your might," as "David danced before the Lord with all his might," came easier, as I returned to the way of music and learned to bring together the way of music and the way of words. It is true, I did not sing and dance myself but only played the piano, having students at Notre Dame do the singing and the dancing. Composing the words and the music, nevertheless, as well as playing the piano, I felt a fire in me that I think is loving "with all your might." It was a response to a dream I had where I heard the words of a command, "Explore the realm of music!" At first I thought to take this metaphorically as a command to explore the realm of feeling, but eventually I took it to mean what it said, "Explore the realm of music!"

Another dream is the beginning of my next book, *Love's Mind*, named for a phrase in *A Midsummer Night's Dream*, and I call the dream there "A Late Summer Night's Dream." In this one I met Saint Thomas Aquinas in the mountains and I asked him "Do we love with a love we know or with a love we do not know?" and he replied "With a love we do not know." It is after this point that I began to speak that way, to say we love with a love we do not know, meaning we are in love with God and do not realize it. I thought of a conversation I had once with a man who was Vietnamese and who had been brought up as a Buddhist but converted to Catholicism at an early age. He told me he saw more in Buddhism now than when he was a Buddhist, especially the reverence for life and the compassion for all living beings, but in Christianity now he saw that you could have "a personal relation with the Absolute"—those were his words—"you could be a friend of God, even" (he added in a whisper) "a lover of God."

Coming to realize the love, to know the love of God then, is what the contemplative life is about, I saw, and I named the book "an essay on the contemplative life," beginning with a chapter on "The Friends of God" and ending with a chapter on "The Lovers of God." I had been giving retreats for monks in Trappist monasteries at Gethsemane and Lafayette and Conyers and Spencer, also at the Camaldolese monastery at Big Sur and at the Carmel in Elysburgh. I saw the monastery as a place like Rivendell in Tolkien's stories, "a perfect house, whether you like food or sleep, or story-telling or singing, or just sitting and thinking best, or a pleasant mixture of them all— Merely to be there was a cure for weariness, fear, and sadness."[6] As I write this I see I am ignoring the severity of the monastic life—above the entrance to the Abbey of Gethsemane the sign reads "God alone."

When I was leaving Gethsemane, the Abbot, Dom Timothy, asked me what I thought of the life there. I said I was very attracted by it and had asked myself if I should stay, but decided against staying because I saw I need a lot of interaction with people. "Yes," he said, "if you are very inward, you need a lot of interaction with people." I wondered afterward if this meant a monk is outward and comes to the monastery to find a balancing inwardness. At any rate, I saw that the contemplative life is an essential dimension of everyone's life, and that it is the missing dimension in our society. Of the three lives Aristotle speaks of, the life of action, the life of contemplation, and the life of enjoyment, we have the two, action and enjoyment, but we lack the other, contemplation. That, I thought, is why ours is a violent city.

In returning to music in this book, writing a song cycle to Ayasofya, the figure of Holy Wisdom, I was learning, as in *Love's Labour's Lost*, to be "still and contemplative in living art."[7] The melody of the principal song was one I had thought of years before in late teen-age and had originally intended for a Kyrie Eleison in a Mass. Here I set the word Ayasofya to the melody, like an Alleluia in Gregorian chant, and I used a form similar to that of Bach's Prelude in C, sending the melody through a series of harmonic variations.[8] It turned out to be very easy and congenial for a soprano to sing, and sopranos I have had for my song cycles such as Kristen Sullivan and Karen Wonder and Alicia Scheidler have all used the song as a warm-up, taking as it does the whole soprano range, from middle C to high A, with open vowel sounds.

Music somehow replaced travel in my life, when I began to compose again, my song cycles or my song and dance cycles took the place of my journeys into South America and into the Middle East, my ventures into the unknown. I called my next book *The Music of Time*. At that time I thought all the roads in my life were coming together, the road of words which I had taken, the road of music my "road not taken," and the road of spiritual friendship. Before she broke off our relationship, a woman who had been a close friend for many years called our relationship "a spiritual friendship," and I gave my book the subtitle "Words and Music and Spiritual Friendship." But by the time the book appeared the relationship was over, and I was learning detachment in love, learning, as I see it now, to love "with all your soul."

I often repeat that prayer, the last stanza of a mystical song by George Herbert, when I feel sadness or dread,

> Come my joy, my love, my heart,
> such a joy as none can move,
> such a love as none can part,
> such a heart as joys in love,[9]

thinking of the love of God as joy at the thought of God (as Spinoza says), for me joy at the thought of God with me on the journey. The joy of friendship can be moved, the love can be parted, but this joy cannot be moved, this love cannot be parted.

What then of the converging roads? Do they still converge? I think of a saying of Wilhelm Grimm I quoted in that book from a fairy tale discovered in the 1980s, "one human heart goes out to another, undeterred by what lies between."[10] My heart goes out to hers (and perhaps her heart goes out to mine) undeterred by the separation that lies between us. So the convergence still comes about, though not in the way I wanted. I see I am being led, ever more deeply, into the life of the spirit. "God is spirit," as Jesus said to the woman at the well, and God acts spiritually, I have come to believe, kindling our hearts and illumining our minds, and we are incarnate spirits, as comes to light in the mystery of encounter and the mystery of our loneliness, and the life of the spirit is a road that goes ever on.

"God and my heart are weeping together"[11] is another saying I quoted there from the Grimm fairy tale. It goes with the idea that "God is vulnerable." The truth is, nevertheless, I feel a joy underlying all, a joy at the thought of being on a journey with God, the joy that is the love of God. "Music must be treated as all things that are eternal, such as love and understanding," I quoted from the Chinese grandmother of one of my students, "because it is these things that will carry us through the darkness of our lives and the death of our bodies to the moon of everlasting peace." Seeing time as "a changing image of eternity," I found that changing image in music, as if all melodies existed in a Platonic world (I thought especially of the melodies of Gregorian chant) and belong to everyone and not to this or that composer.

Composing the two song cycles at the end of the book, "The Church of the Poor Devil" and "The Golden Key," I drew especially on the melodies of Gregorian chant. These two song cycles, however, were song and dance cycles, not simply song cycles like my first two, "Ayasofya" and "Songs about Songs." I was learning what it is to love "with all your might," I think, as when "David danced before the Lord with all his might." My own part was to compose the words and the music and to play the piano, but I could feel the exultation of the singing and the dancing.

Learning to love, though, "with all your soul," learning detachment in love, as I understood it, was my spiritual problem still and the thing I was wrestling with in my next book, *The Mystic Road of Love.* A friend of mine, reading that book, thought I was returning to the problem of loss in love that I had discussed years before in my Oxford lectures, *The Reasons of the Heart.* She quoted to me the passage in Deuteronomy, "You must never go back that way again."[12] And it is true, I began the book with a song I had written for a new song cycle, "The Green Child,"

> Once upon
> a time of loss
> I set out on a mystic
> road of love.[13]

All the same, I was trying there to reenact Dante's journey in *The Divine Comedy,* going from being "lost in a dark wood" to being caught up in "the love that moves the sun and the other stars." Instead of three parts, hell and purgatory and heaven, I envisioned two, the part where Virgil is guide and that where Beatrice is guide. I called the first "The Way Below" and took as my guide the Virgil in Hermann Broch's *Death of Virgil,* and I called the second "The Way Above" and took as my guide Ayasofya, the figure of Holy Wisdom. My own experience of being "lost in a dark wood" was the beginning of "The Green Child" where I sing of "a time of loss," and my own experience of being caught up in "the love that moves the sun and the other stars" is the ending of the other song cycle there, "The Well at the World's End," where I sing "all our loves are one love."[14]

What I learned from Broch's Virgil, going with him through water and fire and earth and air, was to find the word at the end ("it was the word beyond speech") as well as in the beginning ("In the beginning was the Word"), the word of life and light and love. I thought of Simon Peter saying to Jesus, "Lord, to whom shall we go? You have the words of eternal life."[15] What I learned from Ayasofya then were "the words of eternal life." I was trying to learn detachment in love, and "the words of eternal life" were the words that gave me the power of detachment, the power of letting be and being open to the mystery, the words that speak of the great circle of life and light and love.

At the end of the book I included my little physical theory, that matter is a dimension. That may seem to have nothing to do with all this, but to me it was very relevant. For if I say "matter is a dimension," I am saying at the other end of things "God is spirit." For a materialist matter is reality and to say it is a dimension makes no sense. If I do say matter is a dimension, then I am saying reality is what is in the dimensions of space and time and matter, namely events, and also what is above and beyond the dimensions, namely spirit. I am saying matter situates as well as being situated in space and time. Thus, for instance, the brain is matter and situates the mind: the brain itself is not the mind but situates the mind, while the mind itself is spirit. Speaking this way, I am in the company of Plato and Augustine and Descartes (!)

Thinking of "the words of eternal life" and "God is spirit" and seeing things in terms of the great circle of life and light and love, I wrote my next book, *Reading the Gospel*. It was primarily about the Gospel of John but also about Matthew, Mark, and Luke, and its method was *lectio divina*, "divine reading," the monastic method of meditation on scripture, letting the words speak to the heart. Years before I had written about the turning points in the life of Jesus in *A Search for God in Time and Memory* and also in a *Commonweal* article

"The Human God: Jesus,"[16] and I had thought of writing a life of Jesus. But I had always seen us entering into the relation of Jesus with his God, and now I was beginning to see this as what is called "the essence of Christianity."

"We can know more than we can tell,"[17] as Michael Polanyi says. We can tell *the story*, and I do in this book, in a chapter called "Turning Points." But we can know more, *the relation*, and that is by entering into the relation of Jesus with his God. It is by dwelling in the particulars of what we know, Polanyi says, that we can know more than we can tell. And that is how it is here, I think, by dwelling in the particulars of the relation of Jesus with his God, Abba, the particulars that are mentioned in the Lord's Prayer (and again in the prayer of Jesus at the Last Supper in John 17), the name Abba, the kingdom, the will, the bread, the forgiveness, the guiding and guarding from temptation and evil. And that dwelling is indwelling, "I in them, and thou in me,"[18] Jesus in the disciples, "I in them," and Abba in Jesus, "and thou in me."

I take it then that there are two aspects of presence here, *I and thou* and *indwelling*, the two coming together in the formula "I in them, and thou in me." I know that "deconstruction," as put forward by Paul DeMan and Jacques Derrida, is a critique of "the metaphysics of presence." I see an answer to this in George Steiner's *Real Presences*,[19] and that is what I find in reading the Gospel, real presences. I know too that the Jesus Seminar has taken the apocryphal *Gospel of Thomas* as the norm for reading the Gospel, but I take instead the Gospel of John as the norm, and I see even in the parables of Matthew and Mark and Luke, and in the turning points of the life of Jesus, going into solitude, returning to the human circle, and going through death to life, the vision of the great circle of life and light and love coming from God and returning to God.

I find in this "the simplicity of vision," as Pierre Hadot calls it, and I tried to express this in the song cycle at the end of the book, "Songlines of the Gospel," named after *The Songlines* by Bruce Chatwin which is about the songlines across aboriginal Australia.[20] My song cycle is a lyrical commentary on the Gospel of John, and I wanted to perform it before the book came out, but my heart surgery (on Valentine's Day !) prevented me from putting it on until the fall after the book had come out.

I have still another book written, but at the time of this writing unpublished, on the cycles of story and song. Here again I think of "the simplicity of vision," seeing all in a great circle of life and light and love. For I see four cycles, the first when all things were at one and we knew "the language of the birds," the second when the human race emerged and separated into peoples at war and at peace, the third our own epoch when the individual has emerged and separated and feels the deep loneliness of the human condition and the longing to be un-alone, and the fourth, still to come, when there will be a reunion of humanity and of all living beings, a reunion with God. I saw a parallel in those cycles with Vico's *corso* and *ricorso,* and I read with delight what he had to say on "poetic wisdom."

Last night in the wee hours a thought came to me, to trust God beyond my own understanding of God. According to my own understanding, God is spirit and acts spiritually, illumining the mind and kindling the heart. But the thought that came to me was to trust God beyond this understanding of mine. As Patricia McKillip has the High One say in a story, "Beyond logic, beyond reason, beyond hope. Trust me."[21] My own vision then of the *corso* as one of emergence and separation points on to a *ricorso* of reunion, and I think it is true, as far as it goes, but it is "poetic wisdom," and I have to look to the higher wisdom of *The Cloud of Unknowing,* and to unknow all I know of

God and of myself, and let God reveal God to me and let God reveal me to me. It is in "the cloud of unknowing" that "a soul is oned with God."[22] Here is the true reunion with God.

I thought at first to describe the cycles of story and song in terms of words and music and to call my book *The Music of Words* to suggest the original unity and the final reunion of words and music. Later I thought to call it *Great Circle of Song,* and finally, considering the road imagery of the chapters, "The Road of Origin," "The Road of Individuation," "The Road of Reunion," I called it *The Road of the Heart's Desire.*[23] I kept a chapter, though, called "The Music of Words" and a short opening chapter called "Waymarks." At the end I have two songcycles, "The King of the Golden River," based on a story by John Ruskin, and "East of the Sun, West of the Moon," based on a Norwegian fairy tale. At this time I've so far composed the music for only one song, really a dance or perhaps five dances from "The King of the Golden River."

"We never come to thoughts," Heidegger says. "They come to us."[24] That is the way it was with the thought that came to me in the wee hours, to trust God beyond my own understanding of God. The very next day and the day after I shared the thought with the young people I was teaching, and then I shared it with two friends my own age, and one said to trust God beyond our own understanding is what is required of us in dying, for our own understanding cannot penetrate the veil of death. I read Tolkien with hope (I read this passage that night):

That night they heard no noise. But either in his dreams or out of them, he could not tell which, Frodo heard a sweet singing running in his mind: a song that seemed to come like a pale light behind a grey rain-curtain, and growing stronger to turn the veil all to glass and silver, until at last it was rolled back, and a far green country opened before him under a swift sunrise.[25]

That was "poetic wisdom," I know, but the thought that had come to me, to trust God beyond my own understanding, may have been God revealing God to me and God revealing me to me.

And now I come at last to the book I am writing now, this auto-biography, *A Journey with God in Time.* I have learned, writing this autobiography, that my life is about learning to love "with all your heart, and with all your soul, and with all your might." What I learned first was to love, as the Gospels add, "with all your mind." That, as I see it, was a matter of coming to a peaceful vision of everything coming from God and of everything returning to God and of Christ as the Way. That came of reading the *Summa* of Saint Thomas over and over, as I used to do, reading the body of each article but skipping the objections and the answers to the objections, reading just for the vision, "the simplicity of vision," as I learned much later, and the vision of Saint Thomas did have that simplicity for me.

I came to learn then what it is to love "with all your heart" when my life opened up before me all the way to death. That was in my late twenties and early thirties, when I realized my youth was passing. I was writing my first book then, *The City of the Gods*, and coming to my own vision of things and my question "If I must die someday, what can I do to fulfill my desire to live?" My life opening up before me all the way to death left me open and vulnerable to the mystery of encounter with other persons and to the mystery of our loneliness for God. To love "with all your heart" is to have your heart in the en-counter with other persons and in the loneliness for God. My en-counter with death was not complete, though, until my mother died and then my father died. This left me alone and lonely in the prospect of life and death.

It took many years to learn to love "with all your soul," since this requires, as I understand it, a detachment in love. One particular relationship, a long friendship with a woman, was the testing ground of this detachment. I can see my struggle to reach this detachment in love running all the way from *The Reasons of the Heart* (1978) to *The Mystic Road of Love* (1999), over twenty years! I found helpful the terminology Heidegger derived from Meister Eckhart, "letting be" (*Gelassenheit*) and "openness to the mystery." I have had to learn to let this friend be and to be open to the mystery in this friendship. I do feel heart-free now, and so perhaps I have at last learned what it is to love "with all your soul." "Heart-free," that is my language, instead of the traditional language of "detachment." There is heart in heart-free, and there is soul.

To love "with all your might" I take to be musical as in the words "David danced before the Lord with all his might," and so I see myself learning this in my return to music in the last decade. It is true, music is something that goes back to my earliest years, as I was picking out melodies on the piano when I was three years old, and I studied piano all through my school years and clarinet in my teen-age years, and I began composing on the piano when I was a teen-ager, and then I directed our little four-part choir when I was studying in Rome, but it was not until my late years that I began again to compose, to write song cycles and then song and dance cycles, and to perform them with student singers and dancers and myself on the piano. Music then was my "road not taken" and it has rejoined now my road taken, the way of words.

I am intrigued, though, by the connection between words and music, and I begin to believe in the musical origin of language, "In the beginning was the song," and also in the musical consummation of language, that at the end, as in Broch's *Death of Virgil*, you come to "the word beyond speech," and that word is musical, the word in the beginning as well as in the end. I feel like the old man in the last of Thomas Cole's paintings of *The Voyage of Life*, gazing up toward the light, "a sweet singing running in his mind, a song that seemed to come like a pale light behind a grey rain-curtain, and growing stronger to turn the veil all to glass and silver. . . ."

Thomas Cole, *The Voyage of Life: Old Age*, 1842. Courtesy of the National Gallery of Art, Washington, D.C. Copyright © 2003. Ailsa Mellon Bruce Fund 1971.16.4.

Song Cycle:
The Voyage of Life

Of God and the Sparrow

I always thought of you,
my God, in childhood
when I saw a sparrow
—maybe I had heard
not one will fall
upon the ground
without your will,
and now I've heard
only a bird knows how to die,
falling headfirst onto the grass:
we always try to rise
instead unto the light,
and I pray and will pray then,
Light—more light!

The Dreaming Sea

I could never swim
in childhood till I
floated in salt water
on the Gulf of Mexico,
and there I learned to lean
upon the ocean's buoyance
as I lean on you, my God,
and I could feel support
from you as from the sea,
a friendly place,
and I dreamed of myself
as captain of a ship,
until I looked into the quiet eye
of hurricane, the perfect storm.

Of Words and Music

I learned to name
the things of earth
and those of heaven,
things divine and human,
as we talked and walked
along the streambed,
he and I, my grandfather,
now you and I, my God,
then all the names in stories
and in songs without words,
she and I, my mother,
and now you and I, my God,
I learn to love
and listen to compose.

A Hill of Dreams

In my dreaming time
when it was of some use
to wish for what I wanted
I wished to be one in love
with you, my God,
to be one of your friends,
the saints your lovers,
that was my dream
as I sat upon a hilltop
contemplating life ahead,
and city there beneath,
and school behind me,

all the many, all unhappy,
dreaming of the happy few.

Flight from the World

A happy world
is other than the world,
I thought, an otherworld,
and you are wholly other,
I believed, and yet I knew
you are the same,
always the same,
and all in motion comes to rest,
as sparrows fly
and come to rest and nest:
we are too late for gods,
but not for you, my God,
too early then for Being,
yet you are with us.

The Simplicity of Vision

A peaceful vision
of all coming from you
and returning to you
and of Christ the way to you
—that was the answer
to my quest of happiness,
my reading through the *Summa,*
through and through,
looking for vision only

and not then for proof,
a mind intuitive
and not discursive,
I was learning to love you,
my God, with all my mind.

And I Too in Arcadia

We can know more
than we can ever tell of you
in story and in song
indwelling in our life's particulars,
and telling of indwelling
is the method of the Renaissance,
and I too in Arcadia
when sent to Rome to study
learned the method
and the dwelling and the telling,
and I too know more
than I can ever tell—
by dwelling and indwelling
an eternal you and I.

Soliloquy in Rome

May I know me!
May I know thee!
the prayer of
all soliloquy,
and it was mine and is
to learn attention

—Amor/Roma
conquers all—
attention is
the prayer of
soul in waiting
to attain the goal,
your presence
every when and where.

The Mystery of Presence

Your silent presence
is the mystery
of our participation:
you are with us,
we are with you,
I was learning,
I was writing
of your life our inner life,
your light our inner light,
your love our wandering joy,
the deeper life eternal,
our beginning
and our ending
in the singing Word.

On Life Opening Up
All the Way to Death

Memento mori,
Don't forget to die,
for I might just forget

and go on living ever on,
but I remember,
and if I must die someday,
what can I do to satisfy
my heart's desire to live?
—One who believes in me,
you say, though he shall die,
yet shall he live,
and I believe in you,
though I shall die,
yet shall I live.
—*Easter 2001*

Remembering God

Do I remember God?
Yes, I go back in memory
to early scenes and sparrows
and beyond them to a haze
and then to *no I am*,
and I become aware
of my long journey,
I am/you are with me,
always guiding,
always guarding,
kindly shining,
leading me by
one step at a time
out of the heart.
—*Easter 2001*

Passing Over

No and mine
a child will say,
and Yes and yours
I learn to say
as I pass over now
into the peaceful presence
you have left behind you
holy, East and West,
by showing yourself
and withdrawing
in a changing world,
a mystery to us
and to a hungering spirit,
Yes and Mine.

O Lord, Let It Remain!

Everyone and everything
belonging to a life
shall enter and shall exit,
O Lord, let something remain!
the singer sings,
resumes the tale,
remembering things past
and dreaming things to come,
but there is hope,
and there is peace,
and there are friends
and understanding,

all the life of spirit,
Lord, let it remain!

"Faith Is God Sensible to the Heart"

You are sensible
to my heart
and that is my faith,
for my life is a journey
and you are my one companion
—so I thought when setting out
upon a journey all alone
—it was my loneliness
that made you sensible
and loneliness can turn to love
when it gives way to joy
at the very thought of you,
the wandering joy
of God-with-us upon the way.

Do Not Be Afraid

There are two eyes
of vision:
one sees human suffering,
the other our heart's longing,
and so do not be afraid
of Freud and Marx,
I told myself,
but just believe

heart speaks to heart,
for you, Lord, are the cry
of the oppressed,
heart of a heartless world,
soul of soulless conditions,
the religion of the poor.

Ayasofya

Wisdom of God,
be with me,
always at work in me,
I pray, Ayasofya,
and I sing of peace
and presence there,
a church a thousand years,
a mosque five hundred years,
and now an empty monument,
empty and full
of all those prayers,
a center of stillness
surrounded by the silence
we all have within.

Wisdom of the Desert

I am happy here,
but if I saw Jerusalem,
I'd not be happy anymore,
our desert guide was saying,
and a young girl with her veil

was happy playing on her flute
with all her flock of goats
        behind,
and she said too by her farewell
that she would not be happy
if she came with us
—how many children do you
        have?
a desert woman asked me
(was I happy?) I said Many,
for love is of you, my God.

Christ Dwells in You As You

I am, you say
and mean the presence,
God-with-us,
and I am dwelling in you,
and I am, I can say too,
and I will die,
but you are dwelling in me
and so I will live,
and what am I to make
of your indwelling presence
if not to believe
you dwell in me as me
and cut through all the
        loneliness
that separates us still?

"Getting Rid of What You Haven't Got"

I must get rid
of what I haven't got,
the love I haven't got,
to find the love I have,
the love of you, my God,
my primal dream,
to be in love with you,
that's what I really want,
and it is easy to love you,
to feel the joy,
if I only let it come,
a joy no one can take away,
a love no one can part,
the music of my heart.

Eternal Music

Time is a changing
image of eternity,
and music is
a changing image
of eternal music:
I will sing
and make my music
for you, O my God,
for this world is a city
full of straying streets,

songlines diverging
and converging,
I will sing of the great circle
of your life and light and love.

Love's Road

Do not seek death.
Death will find you.
But seek the road which
makes death a fulfillment,

You said to Dag,
You say to me,
and which is that way
if not love's road with you,
the mystic road of love,
the low road of our loneliness
becoming love and joy,
and the high road of our friendship
coming to the love
that moves the sun and stars.

Notes

A Storyboat

1. Ursula K. LeGuin, *A Fisherman of the Inland Sea* (New York: Harper Prism, 1994), p. 159.

2. Marie Louise von Franz quotes this from a conversation with Jung in her preface to *Aurora Consurgens* (ascribed to Saint Thomas Aquinas), trans. R. F. C. Hull and A. S. B. Glover (New York: Random House/Pantheon, 1966), p. xiii. See my discussion in *The Homing Spirit* (New York: Crossroad, 1987, rpt. Notre Dame, Ind.: University of Notre Dame Press, 1997), p. 15.

3. Michael Polanyi, *The Tacit Dimension* (Gloucester, Mass.: Peter Smith, 1983), p. 4.

4. A song from my songcycle "Ayasofya" in my book *Love's Mind* (Notre Dame, Ind.: University of Notre Dame Press, 1993), p. 129.

5. Matthew 10:29 and Luke 12:6 (King James).

6. Genesis 1:3 (King James).

7. Ray Bradbury, *Dandelion Wine* (New York: Bantam, 1969), p. 2.

8. Ecclesiastes 1:5 (It is the title of Ernest Hemingway's first novel).

9. Ludwig Wittgenstein, *Tractatus Logico-Philosophicus,* trans. D. F. Pears and B. F. McGuinness (London: Routledge & Kegan Paul, 1961), p. 149 (#6.45).

10. Bradbury, *Dandelion Wine,* p. 7.

11. Genesis 5:24 (RSV).

12. Muriel Rukeyser, "This Place in the Ways," in John Ciardi, ed., *Mid-Century American Poets* (New York: Twayne, 1950), p. 57.

13. J. R. R. Tolkien, *The Lord of the Rings* (one-volume edition) (London: George Allen & Unwin, 1969), p. 739.

14. Genesis 2:17 and 3:4.

15. Tolkien, *Lord of the Rings,* p. 739.

16. Ascribed to Aquinas in George N. Shuster, *Saint Thomas Aquinas* (New York: Heritage, 1971), p. 3.

17. The translation cited by Shuster is from Thomas Gilby, *Saint Thomas Aquinas: Philosophical Texts* (New York: Oxford University Press, 1960), p. 2 (#3). The Latin original is in *Sancti Thomae Aquinatis Opera Omnia,* vol. 6, ed. Robert Busa (Stuttgart: Frommann-Holzboog, 1980), p. 48 (the prologue to his commentary on the Psalms).

18. Tolkien, *Lord of the Rings,* p. 87.

19. I have the melody in my book *Love's Mind,* p. 48.

20. A friend quoted this saying of Disraeli's in a letter, but I have been unable to find it in his writings, but I did find these lines

Alas for those that never sing,
But die with their music in them

in Oliver Wendell Holmes, "The Voiceless," in his *Poetical Works,* vol. 1 (Boston and New York: Houghton Mifflin, 1892), p. 247.

21. "Everyman" in *Earlier English Drama,* ed. F. J. Tickner (London and Edinburgh: Nelson, 1926), p. 240, quoted in my *Mystic Road of Love* (Notre Dame, University of Notre Dame Press, 1999), p. 39.

22. Dag Hammarskjöld, "A Room of Quiet: The United Nations Meditation Room" (New York: United Nations, 1971), p. 1.

A Quest of Happiness

1. Wittgenstein, *Tractatus*, p. 147 (#6.43).
2. Shakespeare, *1 Henry IV*, act 2, scene 4, line 359 in *The Pelican Shakespeare*, ed. Alfred Harbage (Baltimore: Penguin, 1969), p. 685. See my discussion in *Love's Mind*, pp. 60–63.
3. Leo Tolstoy, *Anna Karenina*, trans. Aylmer Maude (New York: Norton, 1970), p. 1.
4. Martin Heidegger, *Discourse on Thinking*, trans. John M. Anderson and E. Hans Freund (New York: Harper & Row, 1966), p. 55.
5. Nikos Kazantzakis, *The Odyssey: A Modern Sequel*, trans. Kimon Friar (New York: Simon & Schuster, 1958), book XVI, line 959.
6. John 8:12 (RSV) in Thomas à Kempis, *The Imitation of Christ*, trans. Leo Sherley-Price (New York: Penguin, 1952), p. 27.
7. Shakespeare, Sonnet 107:2 in Shakespeare, *Complete Sonnets* (New York: Dover, 1991), p. 47.
8. See Gilbert Keith Chesterton, *Saint Francis of Assisi* (New York: Doran, 1924), pp. 19–24.
9. See Chesterton, *Saint Thomas Aquinas* (New York: Doubleday, 1956), pp. 120–143.
10. John Henry Newman, "Knowledge Viewed in Relation to Learning" in his *Idea of a University*, ed. Charles Frederick Harold (New York: Longmans, 1947), pp. 110–133.
11. Søren Kierkegaard, *Philosophical Fragments*, trans. David Swenson and Howard Hong (Princeton, N.J.: Princeton University Press, 1962), p. 53.
12. From my song cycle "Songs about Songs" in *Love's Mind*, pp. 134–135.
13. Felix Mendelssohn-Bartholdy, *Songs without Words*, ed. Constantin von Sternberg (New York/London: Schirmer, 1915).
14. See *The New Science of Giambattista Vico*, trans. Thomas Goddard Bergin and Max Harold Fisch (Ithaca and London: Cornell University Press, 1994), book two: Poetic Wisdom, pp. 109–297.

15. Henry Chadwick, *Saint Augustine's Confessions* (Oxford: Oxford University Press, 1991), p. xxiv.

16. See my discussion of this idea in *The Mystic Road of Love*, pp. 137–141.

17. John 4:24 (RSV).

18. Quoted by Loren Eisely, *The Night Country* (New York: Scribner's, 1971), p. 166.

19. Dante, *Inferno*, canto 1, lines 2–3 (my trans.).

20. Dante, *Paradiso*, canto 33, line 145 (my trans.).

21. See my discussion of this sentence in my *Church of the Poor Devil* (New York: Macmillan, 1982; rpt. Notre Dame: University of Notre Dame Press, 1983), p. 111.

An Italian Journey

1. Hebrews 13:14 (KJ).

2. Edward Gibbon, *Autobiography*, ed. M. M. Reese (London: Routledge & Kegan Paul, 1970), p. 85.

3. Goethe, *Italian Journey*, trans. W. H. Auden and Elizabeth Mayer (London: Penguin, 1970), p. 21.

4. See Christopher Dawson, *Religion and Culture* (New York: Sheed & Ward, 1948).

5. Shakespeare, *Timon of Athens*, act 5, scene 1, line 200 in *The Pelican Shakespeare*, p. 1166.

6. Virgil, *Aeneid* VI, line 126 (my trans.). I am using the text in *Virgil*, ed. H. Rushton Fairclough, vol. 1 (Cambridge, Mass.: Harvard University Press, 1960), p. 514.

7. Martin Heidegger, *Poetry, Language, Thought*, trans. Albert Hofstadter (New York: Harper & Row, 1971), p. 4.

8. Goethe, *Italian Journey*, p. 376.

9. Goethe, *The Flight to Italy: Diary and Selected Letters*, trans. T. J. Reed (Oxford: Oxford University Press, 1999), p. 140.

10. See my discussion of this idea in my *Church of the Poor Devil*, p. 136, and in the summary of my dissertation cited below in note 19.

11. Jean Leclercq, *The Love of Learning and the Desire for God*, trans. Catharine Misrahi (New York: Fordham University Press, 1982). See my discussion in *Reading the Gospel* (Notre Dame: University of Notre Dame Press, 2000), p. 21.

12. The phrase "with all your mind" is added in the Gospels (Matthew 22:37, Mark 12:29–30, Luke 10:27) (RSV) to "with all your heart, and with all your soul, and with all your might" in Deuteronomy 6:4–5 (RSV). See my *Reading the Gospel*, p. 74.

13. See my discussion of Saint Thomas's saying *Nullum, Domine, nisi teipsum* in *House of Wisdom* (San Francisco: Harper & Row, 1985; rpt. Notre Dame: University of Notre Dame Press, 1993), p. 16.

14. Kings 3:5 (RSV). See my discussion in *House of Wisdom*, p. 2.

15. Matthew 6:13 in the King James Version.

16. Polanyi, *The Tacit Dimension*, p. 4 (cited above in "A Storyboat," n. 3).

17. Wittgenstein, *Tractatus Logico-Philosophicus*, p. 149 (#6.44), cited above in "A Storyboat," n. 9. See my discussion in *The Mystic Road of Love*, p. 82.

18. 2 Peter 1:4 (KJ).

19. See my summary of my dissertation, "St. Thomas' Theology of Participation" in *Theological Studies* (December 1957), pp. 487–512.

20. See Bernard J. F. Lonergan, *Insight* (London: Longmans, 1957), pp. 348–350.

21. Genesis 3:7 (KJ and RSV).

To Choose/to Discover the Way

1. Jean-Paul Sartre, *Essays in Existentialism*, ed. Wade Baskin (New York: Citadel, 1993) (reprint), p. 34.

2. See Karl Barth, *Anselm: Fides Quaerens Intellectum* (New York: Meridian, 1962).

3. Søren Kierkegaard, *Concluding Unscientific Postscript,* trans. David Swenson and Walter Lowrie (Princeton: Princeton University Press, 1941), p. 15.

4. See my discussion of these four sentences in *The House of Wisdom,* where these four sentences are chapter titles.

5. *The City of the Gods* (New York: Macmillan, 1965; rpt. Notre Dame: University of Notre Dame Press, 1978).

6. John 6:68 (RSV).

7. John 11:25–26 (my trans.).

8. Dag Hammarskjöld, *Markings,* trans. Leif Sjöberg and W. H. Auden (New York: Knopf, 1964), p. 159.

9. Saint Augustine, *Soliloquies,* book 2, chapter 1 (my translation of *noverim me, noverim te*).

10. *The Cloud of Unknowing,* trans. Clifton Wolters (New York: Penguin, 1978), p. 105 (end of chapter 37).

11. Saint Augustine, *Confessions,* book 1, chapter 1.

12. *Search for God in Time and Memory* (New York: Macmillan, 1969; rpt. Notre Dame: University of Notre Dame Press, 1977).

13. "There is no disciple at second hand" Kierkegaard says in *Philosophical Fragments*, p. 131.

14. T. S. Eliot, *Four Quartets* (San Diego, New York, London: Harcourt Brace Jovanovich, 1988), pp. 23 and 32 (first and last lines of "East Coker").

15. André Malraux, *Anti-Memoirs,* trans. Terence Kilmartin (New York: Holt, 1968), p. 2. See my discussion in *The Way of All the Earth,* (New York: Macmillan 1972; rpt. Notre Dame: Notre Dame Press, 1978), p. 3.

16. Martin Buber, *I and Thou,* trans. Ronald Gregor Smith (New York: Scribner's, 1958), p. 66.

17. Gandhi called his autobiography *The Story of My Experiments with Truth* (Boston: Beacon, 1957).

18. *The Way of All the Earth* is cited in n. 15 above. The phrase is from Joshua 23:14 and 1 Kings 2:2 (KJ).

19. John Henry Newman, *Prose and Poetry*, ed. George N. Shuster (New York: Allyn & Bacon, 1925), p. 116.

20. Robert Frost, "The Road Not Taken" in *Complete Poems of Robert Frost* (New York: Holt, 1949), p. 131.

21. See B. F. Skinner, *Science and Human Behavior* (New York: Macmillan, 1953), pp. 283–294 on "self."

22. B. F. Skinner, *Particulars of My Life* (New York: Knopf, 1976). See above on Shakespeare in "A Quest of Happiness," n. 2.

The Mystery of Encounter

1. Paul Celan, *Collected Prose*, trans. Rosemarie Waldrop (Manchester: Carcanet, 1986), p. 49.

2. Tolkien, *Lord of the Rings*, p. 292.

3. Dunne, *Time and Myth* (New York: Doubleday, 1973; rpt. Notre Dame: University of Notre Dame Press, 1975), p. 79.

4. Ibid., p. 70.

5. Tolkien, *Lord of the Rings*, p. 383.

6. *The Cloud of Unknowing*, pp. 66–67 (chapter 5). See my *Homing Spirit*, p. 17.

7. Dunne, *Homing Spirit*, p. 20.

8. Ibid., p. 10.

9. Ibid., p. 8.

10. Ibid., p. 32.

11. Matthew 15:14. See my *Homing Spirit*, p. 53.

12. "Blind and Seeing" in my songcycle "Songlines of the Gospel" in *Reading the Gospel*, p. 143.

13. Dunne, *Reasons of the Heart* (New York: Macmillan, 1973; rpt. Notre Dame: University of Notre Dame Press, 1979), p. 1.

14. Ibid., p. 2.

15. Ibid., p. 96.

16. Ibid., p. 144 and p. xii.

17. Ibid., p. 5.

18. Martin Heidegger, *Discourse on Thinking,* p. 55.

19. Dunne, *Reasons of the Heart,* pp. 72–73 (on "soul"), 94–100 ("He who finds his soul will lose it"), and 111-116 ("He who loses his soul for my sake will find it").

20. Dunne, *Homing Spirit,* pp. 7 and 31.

21. Buber, *I and Thou,* trans. Ronald Gregor Smith (New York: Scribner's, 1958), p. 66.

22. Dunne, *Reasons of the Heart,* pp. 122–129 (John 17:23 RSV).

23. Dunne, *Church of the Poor Devil,* p. 157, n. 1.

24. Tolkien, *Lord of the Rings,* p. 1122.

25. Karl Marx, *Critique of Hegel's Philosophy of Right,* ed. Joseph O'Malley (Cambridge: Cambridge University Press, 1970), p. 131. See my *Church of the Poor Devil,* p. viii.

26. See my *Reading the Gospel,* p. 108.

The Mystery of Our Loneliness

1. Shakespeare, *All's Well That Ends Well,* act 1, scene 3, line 179 in *The Oxford Shakespeare* (London: Oxford University Press, 1957), p. 274.

2. See my *House of Wisdom,* pp. 123 and 153.

3. Ibid., p. 56, n. 24, and p. 55, n. 21.

4. Saint Thomas Aquinas, *Summa Theologiae,* part 3, question 23, article 2, *Sed Contra* (Rome: Editiones Paulinae, 1962), p. 1983.

5. Proverbs 9:1 (RSV).

6. See my *House of Wisdom,* p. 162.

7. Ibid., p. ix.

8. Ibid., p. xi.

9. 1 Kings 9:3 and 2 Chronicles 7:16 (RSV), the epigraph of my *House of Wisdom.*

10. John G. Neihardt, *Black Elk Speaks* (Lincoln: University of Nebraska Press, 1961), p. 198.

11. Jean Giono, *The Man Who Planted Trees,* with an afterword by Norma L. Goodrich (Chelsea, Vt.: Chelsea Green, 1985), p. 50.

12. It was originally published in *Vogue* in 1954 as "The Man Who Planted Hope and Grew Happiness."

13. Plotinus, *Enneads* 6:9. See my discussion in my *Mystic Road of Love,* p. 50 and n. 91 on p. 150.

14. See my discussion, ibid., p. 61.

15. Tolkien, *Lord of the Rings,* pp. 1010–1011.

16. John 20:17 (RSV).

17. George Bernard Shaw, *Man and Superman,* act 4

18. Tolstoy as quoted by Max Gorky, *Reminiscences of Tolstoy, Chekhov, and Andreev,* trans. by Katherine Mansfield, S. S. Koteliansky, and Leonard Wolff (London: Hogarth, 1948), p. 23. See my discussion in *Love's Mind,* p. 60.

19. Larry McMurtry, *Crazy Horse* (New York: Penguin, 1999), p. 51.

20. See my discussion and song in *The Mystic Road of Love,* pp. 116–117.

21. From *Welcome to the Monastery of St. Macarius* (by Matta el-Meskeen) at Scetis (Wadi Natrun) in Egypt, printed at the monastery in 1983, p. 7.

22. 1 Peter 5:11 (KJ).

23. Tolkien, "On Fairy-Stories" in *The Tolkien Reader* (New York: Ballantine, 1991), p. 52.

24. Shakespeare, *The Tempest,* act 1, scene 1, lines 19–25 as epigraph of my book, *The Peace of the Present* (Notre Dame: University of Notre Dame Press, 1991), p. vii.

25. Mark 6:50 (RSV and my trans.).

26. Galatians 2:20 (RSV). The inaugural lecture I mention was on the occasion of my inauguration to the John A. O'Brien Chair in theology at Notre Dame on April 18, 1989.

27. Tolkien, *Lord of the Rings,* p. 789.

The Road That Goes Ever On

1. Tolkien, *Lord of the Rings*, p. 87. Quoted above in "A Storyboat," n. 18.

2. Psalm 90:10. I am quoting from the Liturgy of the Hours for Morning Prayer on Monday of Week IV.

3. 2 Samuel 6:14 (RSV).

4. Reiner Schürmann, *Meister Eckhart* (Bloomington: Indiana University Press, 1978), p. xiv.

5. Kathleen Norris, *Dakota* (New York: Ticknor & Fields, 1993), p. 102.

6. Tolkien, *Lord of the Rings*, p. 241.

7. Shakespeare, *Love's Labour's Lost*, act 1, scene 1, line 14 in *The Oxford Shakespeare*, p. 144.

8. I have the melody in my *Love's Mind*, p. 48.

9. From George Herbert's poem "The Call" set to music by Ralph Vaughan Williams in his song cycle "Five Mystical Songs" (1911).

10. Wilhelm Grimm, *Dear Mili*, trans. Ralph Manheim with pictures by Maurice Sendak (New York: Farrar Straus & Giroux, 1988), no page numbering. I quote it in *The Music of Time* (Notre Dame: University of Notre Dame Press, 1996), p. 63.

11. Ibid., I quote it in *The Music of Time*, p. 62.

12. Deuteronomy 17:16 (Jerusalem Bible).

13. I have this on p. 1 and p. 125 of *The Mystic Road of Love*.

14. Ibid., p. 136.

15. John 6:68 (RSV).

16. See my article "The Human God: Jesus" in *Commonweal* (February 10, 1967), pp. 508–511. See also my book *A Search for God in Time and Memory*, pp. 8–14.

17. Polanyi, *The Tacit Dimension*, p. 4, quoted above in "A Storyboat," n. 3.

18. John 17:23 (RSV).

19. George Steiner, *Real Presences* (Chicago: University of Chicago Press, 1989).

20. Bruce Chatwin, *The Songlines* (New York: Penguin, 1988). See my "Songlines of the Gospel" in my *Reading the Gospel* (Notre Dame: University of Notre Dame Press, 2000), pp. 141–146. Pierre Hadot, *Plotinus or the Simplicity of Vision,* trans. Michael Chase (Chicago: University of Chicago Press, 1993).

21. Patricia McKillip, *Riddle-Master* (New York: Ace, 1999), p. 179.

22. *The Cloud of Unknowing and Other Works,* p. 46.

23. *The Road of the Heart's Desire* (Notre Dame: University of Notre Dame Press, 2002).

24. Heidegger, *Poetry, Language, Thought,* p. 6.

25. Tolkien, *Lord of the Rings,* p. 150.

JOHN S. DUNNE

is the John A. O'Brien Professor of Theology
at the University of Notre Dame.
He is the author of more than fifteen books,
including *The Road of the Heart's Desire, Reading the Gospel,*
and *The Mystic Road of Love,*
all published by the University of Notre Dame Press.